araxi

seasonal recipes from the
CELEBRATED WHISTLER RESTAURANT

JAMES WALT

with contributions from
AARON HEATH & **SAMANTHA RAHN**

text by **JIM TOBLER**

photography by **JOHN SHERLOCK**

DOUGLAS & MCINTYRE
D&M PUBLISHERS INC.
Vancouver/Toronto/Berkeley

Araxi Restaurant
4222 Village Square
Whistler BC VON 1B4
www.araxi.com

Douglas & McIntyre
A division of D&M Publishers Inc.
2323 Quebec Street, Suite 201
Vancouver BC V5T 4S7
www.dmpibooks.com

Library and Archives Canada Cataloguing in Publication
Araxi : seasonal recipes from the celebrated
Whistler restaurant

Contains recipes from the Araxi Restaurant.
Includes index.
ISBN 978-1-55365-367-7

1. Cookery—British Columbia—Whistler.
2. Cookery, Canadian—British Columbia style.
3. Araxi Restaurant. I. Araxi Restaurant

TX715.6.A68 2009   641.509711´33   C2008-908066-1

Editing by Lucy Kenward
Copyediting by Pam Robertson
Jacket and text design by Naomi MacDougall
Jacket photographs by John Sherlock except back jacket
far left image by Randy Lincks, www.randylincks.com
Interior photos by John Sherlock, except pages i and ii
by Randy Lincks, www.randylincks.com, and
pages 131 and 231 © Stuart McCall/North Light
Printed and bound in China by C&C Offset Ltd.
Printed on acid-free paper
Distributed in the U.S. by Publishers Group West

We gratefully acknowledge the financial support of the
Canada Council for the Arts, the British Columbia Arts
Council, the Province of British Columbia through the
Book Publishing Tax Credit and the Government of Canada
through the Book Publishing Industry Development
Program (BPIDP) for our publishing activities.

Contents

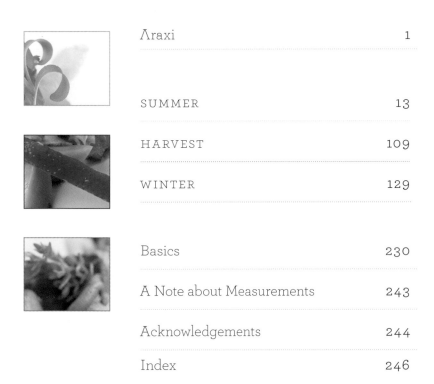

THE PINNACLE Araxi Restaurant sits on what is known as Lot 01 on the main square in Whistler Village. From the front door of the restaurant is a view of the two highest skiable vertical peaks in North America: Whistler and Blackcomb. The marvel is not that they exist, but that they sit side by side, twin peaks in a sublime alpine setting. In 1980, when Whistler Village was nothing more than a gleam in people's eyes, there were only a few recently begun excavation sites, some modest accommodations, a small handful of eateries and, of course, ardent skiers.

Today, the community sits at the top of virtually every list of international ski resorts. It is also well established as a year-round resort, with award-winning golf courses and some of the best downhill and cross-country mountain biking terrain in the world.

During a visit from Montreal, where he was living, owner Jack Evrensel fell in love with Whistler and chose it as the site for his first restaurant venture, Araxi. The restaurant is aptly named for his wife. "What drew us here was the promise of what the village could be," he says. "Two majestic mountains side by side with a twenty-first-century alpine village built right at their base. The architecture, drawing from historic ski villages, inspired by the supernatural surroundings and with an eye towards the future." The view of the mountain peaks from the restaurant's front doors has inspired Araxi's mantra to represent the best that the region offers. Much like Whistler itself, Araxi has always embodied the serene, magical, natural environment surrounding it.

Araxi officially opened October 31, 1981. "From the first day it was clear Jack would drive the place in a certain direction," says Tim Pickwell, who was part of that opening team and still works at the restaurant as sous-chef. "With all the attention to detail, we were making Araxi better every single day. It meant we very quickly became very good at what we were doing."

Chef James Walt was a star on the rise when he first arrived at Araxi in 1997. A young executive chef with talent and ambition, James was a graduate of the prestigious Stratford Chefs School and fresh off a four-year tenure at Sooke Harbour House, which was a mecca for organic, regional cuisine. He had firm ideas about the food he wanted to cook, and Araxi would prove the perfect fit, not only because the restaurant allowed him to showcase regional foods but also because of the bounty he soon discovered in the farmlands beyond Whistler Village. Critical acclaim soon followed. The reviewer for *The Times of London* wrote, "the food was so beautifully attuned to its locale and served in expertly cooked combinations that this was the culinary pinnacle of my trip to B.C. Araxi would surely be showered with Michelin stars, were the award system to operate in Canada."

The restaurant has collected many accolades over the years. The culinary team at Araxi was invited by the James Beard Foundation in New York City to host a dinner representing British Columbia, made not only with the province's indigenous foods but with its premier wine selections as well. The success of the sold-out event sparked two subsequent visits to the much-heralded foundation. In the same period, Araxi won the Gold Award as Best Restaurant in Whistler as voted on by the critics of *Vancouver*

Magazine, beginning an unprecedented run of nine straight wins. However, probably the greatest result of the restaurant's success was its role as the catalyst for one of Canada's most acclaimed and groundbreaking groups of restaurants, the Top Table Group. Jack has since opened CinCin (1991), Blue Water Cafe (2000) and West (2000), all of which are located in downtown Vancouver, 120 kilometres (75 miles) south of Whistler.

Araxi remains a success. Chef Gordon Ramsay rates it as the best in Canada. *Gourmet* magazine asserts, "Araxi has been at the top of the Whistler food scene for 25 years, and after enjoying a few icy shoals of oysters and some meaty Qualicum Beach scallops, I understand why." A look at the restaurant's alumni—Bradley Fraser, Brian Hopkins, Neil Henderson, Andrew Richardson, Chris Van Nus—most of them still working within the Top Table Group, speaks to Araxi's overall commitment to quality. The pursuit of excellence is a constant.

THE CUISINE James Walt, like pastry chef Aaron Heath and sous-chef John Ferris, lives in the Pemberton Valley. The town of Pemberton, which lies a thirty-minute drive north of Whistler, is home to numerous farms, of which two or three are sizable entities. Pemberton is known worldwide for its seed potato crops, since these and other root crops in the valley are entirely free of disease and viruses. The surrounding mountains provide a natural barrier, a shield that protects these vegetables, making them extremely desirable due to their quality.

Araxi's ever-changing menu is inspired by the daily visits the chefs make to these local farms to select produce that is picked fresh each morning: baby arugula and organic salad greens from Across the Creek Organics; asparagus, raspberries, sunchokes or squash blossoms from North Arm Farm near Mount Currie. In addition to produce grown nearby, the kitchen at Araxi makes use of sustainably harvested B.C. fish and shellfish, as well as of fruit, vegetables, nuts and grains grown in the fertile soil of the Fraser Valley and the ever-evolving Okanagan region.

The mandate at Araxi is to handle foods gently and enhance their natural flavours, so the ingredients are the stars. James is always curious, almost studious, in his approach to and his understanding of food. Scallops from Qualicum Beach, sablefish from the deep waters off the east coast of Vancouver Island and beef from Pemberton are found in the kitchen the year through, but they are prepared differently and paired with varying flavours to reflect the seasons in which they are served. Nothing at Araxi is forced, and the menu has its own natural cycle.

In the colder months, James invests many hours hand-picking items from North Arm Farm's storage cellars. He marvels, "What we have stored here is enough root-crop produce to last us the entire winter. It is a tremendous thing, to have sustainable vegetables like this available to us throughout the year." This approach to food is not so far removed from the way the early settlers of this continent grew and either stored or preserved their crops.

Aaron brings the same high level of dedication to the food he prepares. "Dessert is an extension of the overall meal," he exclaims. "You can't be made to feel you've been suddenly transported to a different restaurant when it arrives. It has to make sense in the context of the entire experience. I work very closely with James,

so the meal works together as a whole." Regardless of the season or the dish, the challenge is to provide a decadent experience in taste and texture contrasts, one that differentiates and defines the several flavours clearly.

James continues, "There is always pressure in a fine-dining restaurant. That pressure is to deliver what we as a restaurant hold out as a promise to our guests: that they will have a great experience with us. But the pressure is also fed by the need to improve every step of the way." James looks around the restaurant and concludes, "The best ingredients, almost all of them local. In this setting. It is magical."

PRECISION AND SERVICE Steve Edwards is Araxi's restaurant director. Before taking the helm in Whistler, Steve was the manager at CinCin for three years. While in Vancouver, Steve validated his passion for wine and acquired his diploma from the International Sommelier Guild. He runs the room at Araxi in an

attentive, proactive manner, no detail too slight to be of importance. His passion for making the evening run smoothly, providing the best dining experience possible night in and night out, is palpable.

The service team at Araxi is not only committed to their work, but very well informed. All staff receive thorough training that involves frequent food quizzes, role-playing seminars and extensive wine tutoring. Due to the relaxed and inspiring mountain setting, the service is convivial and energetic. This approach is deliberate, and Steve is thoughtful about it: "Araxi is known to have a diverse clientele, from young local snowboarders to well-travelled billionaires who have dined in some of the best restaurants in the world." Steve continues, "It's our goal to provide the best possible experience we can to every guest who walks through our doors."

Impeccable service tailored to individual guests is also top of mind for Alia Daut-Labesse, the manager of Araxi. She started as the maître d' at West and also spent three years studying at École Wilbrod-Behrer in Quebec City. "You have to make sure that everything is just right," states Alia. Even during the busiest times, the service remains focused, precise and calm. Says Steve, "I absolutely believe we could transport this restaurant to any city in the world and be successful there."

THE WINE Samantha Rahn is Araxi's wine director and she works closely with assistant wine director Pat Allan. One of the great joys of her job is pairing the food with memorable wines drawn from among the restaurant's list of nearly one thousand

labels and over fifteen thousand bottles. "The flavours in James's dishes are so pure and balanced, it makes creating magical pairings for our guests almost easy, and very rewarding," she says. The wine list at Araxi is a perennial winner of *Wine Spectator*'s "Best of" Award of Excellence, in addition to its numerous other awards and critical acclaim.

Building and developing the wine program is a labour of love for Samantha: "Steve, Pat and I always work closely together to source the best wines for Araxi, trophies and treasures alike. Our goal is to always offer tremendous value to our guests, whether they are searching for a specific cult California Cabernet or looking for a new discovery, perhaps a region or a varietal they have not tried before." With Araxi's diverse international clientele, B.C. wines are in high demand, and Samantha and her sommelier team (one of Araxi's crew of certified sommeliers is always on hand) oblige with carefully chosen selections from B.C.'s

fast-growing wine industry. "Okanagan wines have dramatically improved, and I work directly with many producers to showcase their fine wines to our discerning guests. It's exciting to introduce these great local wines to visitors who may not even realize that we make wine in B.C.," Samantha says with pride.

Knowing which wines complement which dishes is a focus of the weekly wine tutorials, which often include seminars and tastings. At Araxi, the staff are trained to know every dish on the menu in depth, and to know which wines would best suit each one. "Everyone is striving to improve, to learn, to create the best guest experience," Samantha says. "James and Steve are great inspirations in driving our team to constantly be better. For me, that means working on the list every day to be sure that we have a perfect balance of styles, prices, rarities, regions—truly something for everyone. I cherish the challenge and take tremendous pride in our collection, and in sharing it with our guests."

THE ROOM AND THE BARS Designed by a renowned Vancouver architect, the late Werner Forster, the main dining room combines warm colours and handsome leather furnishings. Stunning floral arrangements and original artworks deliver an effortless elegance. The windows look out onto the village square, and in the summer months the room is extended to include outdoor dining. The outside tables face southwest so that the sun sets beside the two majestic mountain peaks, capturing the pristine landscape that defines the Sea-to-Sky Corridor. There is also a private wine room whose walls house thousands of bottles from Araxi's acclaimed wine collection.

The bar is a vital and welcoming feature of the main room. It sits immediately left of the entrance and kitty-corner to the Raw Bar. This seafood bar, with its marble and frosted steel counters, was added in 2003 and is an extension of the main kitchen. The goal is to highlight fresh B.C. fish and shellfish, including oysters, by preparing them simply. The main bar has a lounge area that includes an outdoor bar where passersby can enjoy a glass of wine and sample small plates from the menu without ever setting foot inside.

Bar manager Rene Wuethrich trained in Switzerland, and when he arrived at Araxi it was a perfect match, much like the flavours in the cocktails he prepares. Whether he is pouring a flute of champagne, a cocktail made with seasonal ingredients or a rare spirit, every drink is served with grace and aplomb. And the bar at Araxi offers a wide variety of choice. There are many single-batch bourbons, rare single-malt scotches and various other fine potables from around the world. The cocktail list reflects the season,

and all fruit juices are pressed to order, to capture their freshness in the glass. The extensive by-the-glass wine list ensures interesting options as well. "There is a nuanced balance of styles, prices, rarities, region," he says, "truly something for everyone. I cherish the challenge and take tremendous pride in our collection."

Just like Whistler, Araxi is constantly evolving to better provide for its guests. Over the years, the restaurant has often closed briefly in May and October for renovations, or as Jack puts it, "a freshening up." This is not the norm in the restaurant business, but he has always maintained that quality comes first. "We want to show our guests the best of what our region has to offer," he says, which is what Jack had in mind when he first opened Araxi all those years ago. "Araxi today is totally unlike the Araxi of more than twenty-five years ago," Jack exclaims. He pauses and then adds, "But the Araxi of today is here today only. The one constant is change, so by this time next year it will be a bit different, and always that little bit better."

SUMMER

recipes

Summer

ASPARAGUS TIPS poking through the snow at North Arm Farm in Pemberton signal the arrival of spring. Close behind them, once the ice melts on the banks of Pemberton Creek, the sun-seeking shoots of stinging nettle and spicy watercress plants start to emerge. For a kitchen that's as seasonally focused as Araxi's, this change of weather heralds a whole new cycle of menus. Executive chef James Walt declares: "We love the spring. The fishing fleets are heading out, and fresh rhubarb, chives, nettles and sorrel start showing up. These crops are a teaser—they're a sign of good things to come."

As skis and snowboards give way to mountain bikes, barbecues and golf clubs around Whistler, the menu at Araxi shifts to simpler dishes. People are generally more active when it's warmer outside, and summer vegetables such as peas, green beans, zucchini and spinach require very little cooking. Lettuces, arugula, tomatoes, berries and soft herbs need no cooking at all. As a result, says James, "I feel that our menus almost write themselves. We just add whatever produce is local and in season, pick the best quality, prepare it properly and take it off the menu when its season has passed."

Highlights of the spring and summer menus at Araxi include chilled pea soup, grilled asparagus served with a crisp Parmesan-crusted egg and tangy raspberry sablés. These dishes may seem complex, but the preparations are models of simplicity; they are designed to showcase the fresh flavours of each ingredient.

"I really think you can have a taste of summer," continues James. "For example, a tempura zucchini blossom stuffed with ricotta cheese and served with ice-cold gazpacho. This dish can only be made at a certain time of year, and it can only succeed if the natural flavours are allowed to shine through."

Like the arrival of farm-fresh produce, the springtime opening of the wild salmon and halibut seasons is always a popular time in the Pacific Northwest, and Araxi's menu reflects this. May signals the beginning of the six-week spot prawn season and the arrival of fish such as lingcod, rockfish and sole. The restaurant's proximity to the coast allows for daily shipments of just-harvested oysters from aquaculture farms on the Sunshine Coast and Denman and Cortes Islands, as well as regular deliveries of ocean-fresh octopus, sea urchin and neon flying squid, all of which find their way into delicious seasonal dishes.

Pastry chef Aaron Heath uses a similar philosophy in making his desserts. As baskets of freshly picked strawberries, blueberries, blackberries and raspberries arrive at the restaurant, Aaron

has already planned the day's pastries and petits fours. Soon after, he's combining Okanagan stone fruits—such as cherries, peaches, nectarines, apricots and plums—in original desserts that show off the best of the region's flavours. "The floral accents in apricots match really well with our B.C. hazelnuts," he says, "and fresh berries and lavender, used sparingly, on chewy meringue is also a perfect marriage."

In the summer, Whistler is a lively place. The main square is packed with visitors relaxing after a long day of hiking, mountain biking, shopping or soaking up the sun at the beaches along Alta and Lost Lakes. The restaurant, like the village, is abuzz with excited energy and basks in the glow of the holiday crowd. The days are long, the pace is frenetic, the mood is upbeat, and as the crops come and go quickly, the menus change constantly. Welcome to summer at Araxi—where the food is fresh from the farm and the feeling of youth lasts forever.

APPETIZERS AND CANAPÉS

Globe Eggplant *and* Goat Cheese Frittos *with* Olive Tapenade — 20

Crab *and* Avocado Spoons — 23

Chilled English Pea *and* Mint Soup — 24

Grilled Asparagus Salad *with* Sherry Vinaigrette *and a* Crispy Egg — 27

Octopus *with* Chickpea Purée *and* Lemon Vinaigrette — 29

Three Cheese–stuffed Squash Blossoms *with* Gazpacho — 33

Cured Wild Salmon *with* New Potatoes *and* Beet Vinaigrette — 36

Albacore Tuna Tataki *with* Baby Vegetables *and* Nasturtiums — 40

Seafood Ceviche *with* Baby Cucumbers *and* Corn Chips — 42

Spot Prawn Salad *with* Cucumber Broth, Cilantro *and* Arugula — 44

Scallop Tartare *with* Avocado-Citrus Salad *and* Fried Ginger — 46

Heirloom Tomato Salad *with* Buffalo Mozzarella — 49

ENTRÉES

Roasted Lingcod *with* Saffron Potatoes *and* White Asparagus — 50

Wild Salmon *with* Artichoke *and* Vegetable Medley — 52

Prosciutto-wrapped Halibut *with* Littleneck Clam Chowder — 55

Seared Red Tuna *with* Chickpea Panisse *and* Salsa Verde — 58

Herb-crusted Halibut *with* Pea Purée *and* Coriander Vinaigrette — 60

Globe Eggplant *and* Goat Cheese Frittos *with* Olive Tapenade

Serves 6 as a cocktail snack (Yields 20 to 24 pieces)

7 oz	soft goat cheese	200 g
1 tsp	finely chopped mint	5 mL
1	large globe eggplant, unpeeled but trimmed	1
20 to 24	toothpicks	20 to 24
12 cups	olive oil, for deep-frying	3 L
2	egg yolks	2
2 cups	sparkling water, ice cold (San Pellegrino is good)	500 mL
2 cups	all-purpose flour, sifted	480 mL
1 recipe	tapenade (page 238)	1 recipe
3½ Tbsp	vincotto	50 mL
20 to 24 sprigs	fresh basil, for garnish	20 to 24 sprigs

I first tasted this appetizer in Italy and loved it for its simplicity. At Araxi, we've added tapenade for a slightly salty tone that pulls all the elements of this dish together. For an equally tasty alternative, try stuffing the eggplant with sausage meat. And if you cannot find vincotto—a sweet reduced grape must—in an Italian specialty store, use aged balsamic vinegar instead.

IN A MEDIUM bowl, combine goat cheese and mint. Lightly season with salt.

Using either a mandoline or a sharp knife, slice the eggplant as thinly as possible across its width into discs. Arranging the eggplant slices on a baking sheet in batches, place a teaspoon of goat cheese in the centre of each round, then fold each eggplant slice in half, securing it with a toothpick to hold the filling in place.

Fill a deep pot or a wok two-thirds full with olive oil and heat it to 330°F/165°C (use a deep-fat thermometer to check the temperature).

Combine the egg yolks and sparkling water in a stainless steel bowl and mix lightly. Gently stir in flour with a fork until just combined (do not overmix or the coating will become heavy). Working in small batches, dip each fritto in the batter until well coated, then deep-fry until golden and crispy, 2 to 3 minutes per batch. Transfer to paper towels to drain. Repeat with the remaining frittos, then remove and discard the toothpicks. Season the frittos with salt.

TO SERVE Spread the tapenade in a line down the middle
of a serving platter and drizzle with vincotto. Arrange the
frittos on either side of the tapenade, garnish with a sprig
of basil and pass the plate around.

WINE Fiano di Avellino from Campania would be fabulous,
as would other good-quality Italian whites such as Soave
or Friuli Pinot Grigio.

Crab *and* Avocado Spoons

Serves 6 (Yields 24 spoons)

We use a lot of crabs at the restaurant, and we have a large live tank in the kitchen to hold them. One of the easiest dishes we make, these crab spoons are a nice twist on a classic appetizer and they are a great way to start a meal. Yuzu juice is a citrus juice that is available from Japanese grocery stores. If it is not available, substitute 2 parts lemon juice to 1 part lime juice.

YUZU MAYONNAISE In a blender, combine egg yolks, Dijon mustard and yuzu juice on slow speed until emulsified. With the motor running, slowly add grapeseed oil in a thin stream until the mayonnaise becomes thick. Season with salt and white pepper, cover and refrigerate until chilled, about 1 hour. Will keep refrigerated in an airtight container for up to 3 days.

CRAB AND AVOCADO In a medium bowl, combine the crabmeat with the mayonnaise and chives. Season lightly with salt and white pepper. Cover and refrigerate until chilled, about 1 hour.

Halve the avocado lengthwise, then remove and discard the pit. Cut each half in half again lengthwise, then slide a knife just under the skin of each segment and peel it off. Discard the avocado skins. Thinly slice the avocado along its length onto a plate, then squeeze lime juice over the slices so they retain their colour.

TO SERVE Arrange 24 Chinese soup spoons on a serving platter. Using a teaspoon, place a small mound of crabmeat on each spoon. Top each portion with a slice of avocado. Pass around the platter, serving 4 spoons per person.

WINE Try Sancerre or Pouilly-Fumé, but if this dish is passed around as a canapé, bubbles are a must: Blanc de blanc Champagne tops the list.

YUZU MAYONNAISE

2	egg yolks	2
1 Tbsp	Dijon mustard	15 mL
¼ cup	yuzu juice	60 mL
2 cups	grapeseed oil	500 mL

CRAB AND AVOCADO

8 oz	fresh crabmeat, picked over for shells or cartilage	225 g
¼ cup	yuzu mayonnaise	60 mL
1 tsp	finely chopped chives	5 mL
1	ripe avocado	1
1	lime, halved	1

Chilled English Pea *and* Mint Soup

Serves 4 as an appetizer or 12 as an amuse-bouche

¼ cup	unsalted butter	60 mL
1	medium onion, diced	1
2 cloves	garlic, sliced	2 cloves
4 cups	vegetable stock (page 233)	1 L
3 cups	fresh, shelled English peas or thawed frozen peas	720 mL
¼ cup	whipping cream	60 mL
¾ cup	spinach, washed and trimmed	180 mL
4 sprigs	fresh mint, leaves only	4 sprigs
1 bunch	pea tops or mint leaves, for garnish	1 bunch

The season for peas seems to get shorter every year, but this is a great recipe for celebrating when they are available. English peas are also known as garden peas or simply green peas. Mint enhances the sweet pea flavour.

IN A MEDIUM saucepan on medium-low heat, sauté the butter, onions and garlic until the onions are softened and garlic is lightly golden, about 5 minutes. Add the vegetable stock, bring to a boil, then reduce the heat to low and simmer for 10 minutes. Add the peas and cook for 4 to 5 minutes. Remove from the heat and add the cream, spinach and mint. Season lightly with salt.

Fill a large bowl with ice. Allow the soup to cool slightly, then transfer it to a blender and purée until smooth. Strain the soup through a fine-mesh sieve into a bowl. Set the bowl of soup over the ice to chill quickly.

TO SERVE Divide the chilled soup among 4 or 12 small chilled glasses or cups. Garnish with pea tops or mint leaves and serve immediately.

WINE Flavourful soups like this are often best without wine, but a delicate sparkler would be good, as would the complementary flavours of New Zealand Sauvignon Blanc.

Grilled Asparagus Salad *with* Sherry Vinaigrette *and a* Crispy Egg

Serves 4

After a long winter of cellared root crops and endless vegetable peeling, asparagus finally signals the arrival of spring. At the restaurant, we use asparagus from North Arm Farm in the Pemberton Valley, which has some of the best-tasting, freshest asparagus available. This recipe uses curry salt and grilling to highlight the asparagus flavour. Trim asparagus by snapping the spears between your fingers to break the stalks, then use a knife to sharpen them like a pencil.

SHERRY VINAIGRETTE In a small bowl, whisk together the grainy mustard and the sherry vinegar until well combined. Slowly add the grapeseed oil in a thin stream, whisking continuously until the vinaigrette is emulsified. Season with salt and pepper. Will keep refrigerated in an airtight container for up to 5 days.

GRILLED ASPARAGUS Preheat a grill or barbecue to high heat.

Fill a large bowl with ice water. Bring a large saucepan of salted water to a boil on high heat. Add the asparagus and cook for 1 minute. Using tongs, remove the asparagus and plunge them into the ice water to stop the cooking, then arrange them on a tea towel to dry.

In a small bowl, combine the salt and curry powder. In a large shallow bowl, gently toss the asparagus and the olive oil, then sprinkle liberally with the curry salt. Grill the asparagus for 1 to 2 minutes per side, or until lightly charred. Remove from the grill (or barbecue) and keep warm.

continued overleaf...

SHERRY VINAIGRETTE

2 Tbsp	grainy mustard	30 mL
¾ cup	sherry vinegar	185 mL
2 cups	grapeseed oil	500 mL

GRILLED ASPARAGUS

24 spears	asparagus, trimmed	24 spears
1½ tsp	kosher salt	7.5 mL
½ tsp	curry powder	2.5 mL
2 Tbsp	olive oil	30 mL

CRISPY EGGS

⅓ cup	white vinegar	80 mL
6	organic eggs	6
12 cups	peanut or vegetable oil, for deep-frying	3 L
½ cup	whole milk	125 mL
½ cup	all-purpose flour	120 mL
1 cup	dry bread crumbs	240 mL
⅔ cup	grated Parmesan cheese	160 mL

CRISPY EGGS Fill a large bowl with ice water. In a medium saucepan on high heat, heat 12 cups/3 L of water. Add the white vinegar and a pinch of salt and bring to a boil. Reduce the heat to low, or until the water is just simmering. Crack 4 eggs into individual ramekins or coffee cups. Swirl the water with a large spoon, then, one at a time, quickly pour the eggs into the water. Poach each egg for 3 minutes. Using a slotted spoon, transfer the eggs to the ice water to stop the cooking. Once the eggs are cool, trim any ragged edges so the whites form nice rounds. Carefully pat the eggs dry with a tea towel.

Fill a deep pot or a wok to two-thirds full with peanut (or vegetable) oil and heat it to 330°F/165°C (use a deep-fat thermometer to check the temperature). In a small bowl, whisk the remaining 2 eggs with the milk. Combine the flour and a pinch of salt in a second bowl and the bread crumbs and Parmesan cheese in a third bowl. One at a time, carefully dredge the poached eggs in the seasoned flour, then dip them in the beaten egg mixture and coat them with the bread crumb mixture. Deep-fry the eggs for 1 minute until golden brown (the eggs will still be runny inside), then use a slotted spoon to transfer the eggs to a paper towel to drain. Lightly season with salt.

TO SERVE Arrange 6 spears of asparagus on each plate, then drizzle with the vinaigrette. Top each serving with a crispy egg and serve immediately.

WINE Asparagus is known to make wine taste nasty; a New Zealand or Chilean Sauvignon Blanc is best, or try Chinon or B.C. Cabernet Franc for a red.

Octopus *with* Chickpea Purée *and* Lemon Vinaigrette

Serves 6

I like to serve chilled poached octopus in the warmer months. In the winter, we grill it with garlic, olive oil and preserved lemons. The key to either dish is the tenderness of the octopus. The chickpea purée in this recipe is very nice on its own or served with bread. Look for lemon vinegar at fine grocers or substitute 1½ Tbsp/25 mL lemon juice mixed with 1 Tbsp/15 mL white wine vinegar.

OCTOPUS Place the octopus in a colander in the sink and sprinkle liberally with the salt. Using your hands, rub the octopus along the sides of the colander to remove some of the film from the tentacles, then rinse under cold water to remove the salt and the film.

Using a heavy-bottomed pot (fitted with a lid) that is large enough to hold the octopus, heat the olive oil and jalapeño pepper on medium-high heat until the oil is almost smoking. Gently add the octopus and the cork. Shake the pot to ensure the octopus is coated in oil, then cover and reduce the heat to medium-low. Cook for 15 minutes until the octopus begins to release its juices. Reduce the heat to low, shake the pot again to prevent the octopus from sticking and continue cooking for 40 to 50 minutes, or until a knife inserted into the thickest part of the leg comes out easily.

continued overleaf…

OCTOPUS

3 to 4 lbs	whole Pacific octopus, innards removed (thawed, if frozen)	1.4 to 1.8 kg
¼ cup	salt	60 mL
3 Tbsp	olive oil	45 mL
1	red jalapeño pepper, halved lengthwise	1
1	wine cork (a cork helps to tenderize the meat)	1
1 cup	baby herbs, for garnish	240 mL
8 to 10	tomato chips (page 49), for garnish	8 to 10

LEMON VINAIGRETTE

½ cup	extra-virgin olive oil	125 mL
2½ Tbsp	lemon vinegar	40 mL
2½ Tbsp	water	40 mL
1 clove	garlic	1 clove
1 sprig	tarragon, stem and whole sprig okay, only for flavour	1 sprig

Remove the octopus from the pot and allow it to cool. Discard the cooking juices. While the octopus is still slightly warm, use a knife to separate the head from the tentacles. (Reserve the head to grill with olive oil and garlic at another date, or discard it. It will keep refrigerated for 3 to 4 days.) Grasp each tentacle in one hand and, with the other hand, run your fingers along the length of the tentacle to remove the skin and suction cups. Discard the skin and suction cups.

Cut a piece of plastic wrap that is 3 to 4 inches/ 7.5 to 10 cm longer than the longest tentacle. Slightly moisten a clean work surface with water and place the plastic wrap on top, with one long edge toward you. Arrange the tentacles lengthwise, side by side, in the centre of the plastic wrap, alternating the narrow and wide ends of the tentacles to make as even a rectangle as possible. Fold the edge of the plastic wrap nearest you over the tentacles, then tightly roll the tentacles in the plastic wrap to create a log shape. Grasp the plastic wrap at both ends of the log and twist them to make the log as tight as possible. Refrigerate the octopus for at least 8 hours or it is until firm to the touch.

LEMON VINAIGRETTE Combine all of the ingredients in a small jar with a lid and shake well. Will keep refrigerated in an airtight container for up to 2 days.

continued overleaf...

CHICKPEA PURÉE

½ cup	extra-virgin olive oil	125 mL
2 cloves	garlic, minced	2 cloves
1	small onion, minced	1
1 tsp	curry powder	5 mL
2 cups	cooked chickpeas	480 mL
½ cup	vegetable stock (page 233)	125 mL
2 Tbsp	lemon juice	30 mL
1 tsp	tahini paste (page 202)	5 mL
1 Tbsp	chopped chives	15 mL

CHICKPEA PURÉE In a small saucepan, heat the olive oil on medium heat. Add the garlic and onions and sauté until soft and slightly coloured, about 5 minutes. Stir in the curry powder and sauté for 2 minutes, then add the chickpeas and the vegetable stock and cook until heated through, about 5 minutes. Transfer to a food processor. Add the lemon juice and tahini paste, season with salt and white pepper and purée until smooth. If the purée is too thick, add more vegetable stock or water. Refrigerate until chilled, about 30 minutes. If any lumps appear, strain the purée through a fine-mesh sieve. Will keep refrigerated in an airtight container for 2 to 3 days.

TO SERVE Spread 2 spoonfuls of chickpea purée on each of six plates. While it is still wrapped in plastic, slice the octopus in ¼-inch/5-millimetre slices, then remove the plastic wrap. Arrange 3 to 4 slices of octopus on each serving of chickpea purée. Drizzle each plate with some of the vinaigrette and sprinkle with fresh chopped chives. Garnish with baby herbs and tomato chips.

WINE For fun, enjoy Vermentino from Sardinia, a modern white from Greece or a white from Rueda or Rioja in Spain. B.C. Pinot Blanc would be a good local choice.

Three Cheese–stuffed Squash Blossoms *with* Gazpacho

Serves 4 to 6

Jordan Sturdy at North Arm Farm in Pemberton keeps us supplied with fresh squash blossoms all summer long. My own preference is a baby zucchini or pattypan squash blossom but any summer squash blossom will work. To me, the combination of ice-cold gazpacho and crispy hot blossoms is the perfect temperature contrast, and highlights the smells of summer.

GAZPACHO Combine all the ingredients in a stainless steel or glass bowl and refrigerate overnight. Transfer to an electric mixer fitted with a paddle attachment and mix at low speed for 10 minutes (or use a potato masher to crush the ingredients as much as possible). Do not purée the gazpacho, as it will change colour and become bitter. Strain the soup through a medium-fine sieve into a clean bowl and refrigerate for at least 4 hours.

SQUASH BLOSSOMS With a sharp knife, trim the blossom stems to ¼ inch/5 mm and, if the fruit is attached, cut off and discard the end of the fruit and slice the squash once lengthwise to help it cook. Gently open the blossom and cut out the stamen. Brush out any dirt or insects inside the blossom.

In a bowl, combine the 3 cheeses and the riced potato and season lightly with salt and pepper. Allow the stuffing to stand in a warm place until it is soft, then transfer it to a piping bag fitted with a wide nozzle.

continued overleaf...

GAZPACHO

2 ½ lbs	very ripe red tomatoes, roughly chopped	1.1 kg
¼ cup	diced onions	60 mL
1	red bell pepper, seeded and diced	1
1	small cucumber, peeled, seeded and diced	1
1 clove	garlic, minced	1 clove
1 Tbsp	sherry vinegar	15 mL
	Juice of 1 lemon	
1 tsp	kosher salt	5 mL
2 Tbsp	extra-virgin olive oil	30 mL
2 cups	fresh tomato juice (1 ½ lbs/680 g fresh tomatoes, juiced or grated)	500 mL

Insert the tip of the piping bag inside each blossom, filling the blossoms three-quarters full with the cheese mixture. Twist the top of each filled blossom to prevent the stuffing from escaping. Place the filled blossoms on a baking sheet and refrigerate until ready to serve.

Fill a deep pot or a wok two-thirds full with olive oil and heat it to 330°F/165°C (use a deep-fat thermometer to check the temperature).

Combine the egg yolks and sparkling water in a stainless steel bowl and mix lightly. Gently stir in the flour with a fork until just combined (do not overmix or the coating will become heavy). Working in three batches, dip each squash blossom into the batter until well coated, then deep-fry until lightly golden and crispy, about 3 minutes per batch. Transfer to paper towels to drain. Repeat with the remaining blossoms. Lightly season the blossoms with salt.

TO SERVE Arrange 2 spoonfuls of tomato marmalade on each plate and top each serving with 2 to 3 squash blossoms. Serve with very cold gazpacho ladled into individual bowls and served on the side.

WINE New World Sauvignon Blanc or good Mosel Riesling Kabinett are both excellent. Be careful to avoid tart or oaky wines, which take away from the sweet fruit in the gazpacho and the delicate, crispy blossoms.

SQUASH BLOSSOMS

12	summer squash blossoms, with or without baby fruit attached	12
3 oz	soft goat cheese	85 g
3 oz	ricotta cheese, strained overnight to remove moisture	85 g
⅛ cup	grated Parmesan cheese	30 mL
1	medium Yukon Gold potato, cooked and riced through a food mill	1
12 cups	olive oil, for deep-frying	3 L
2	egg yolks	2
2 cups	sparkling water, ice cold (San Pellegrino is good)	500 mL
2 cups	all-purpose flour, sifted	480 mL
¾ cup	tomato marmalade (page 238), for garnish	180 mL

Cured Wild Salmon *with* New Potatoes *and* Beet Vinaigrette

Serves 6

CURED SALMON

¼ cup	kosher salt	60 mL
2 Tbsp	granulated sugar	30 mL
2 Tbsp	ground coriander	30 mL
3 sprigs	fresh dill, washed and stems removed	3 sprigs
1½ lbs	fresh wild salmon fillet, skin on, scaled and pin bones removed	680 g
¼ cup	vodka or aquavit	60 mL

Located as we are on the West Coast, salmon is in high demand among our guests. This dish features not only great fish, but the stellar potatoes and beets for which the Pemberton Valley is known. Fresh beet juice is available commercially but if you have a juicer you can also make your own. The crème fraîche really brings all the flavours together.

CURED SALMON In a small bowl, combine the salt, sugar and coriander. Cut an 11 × 18-inch/30 × 45-cm piece of plastic wrap and place it in the bottom of a shallow dish just large enough to hold the salmon. Allow the edges of the plastic wrap to hang over the sides of the dish. Cut a piece of cardboard to just fit the dish and set aside.

Sprinkle one-third of the dill and one-third of the salt mixture over the plastic wrap, then place the salmon, skin side down, on top. Using a pastry brush, baste the fish with the vodka (or aquavit) and cover it with the remaining salt mixture and dill. Fold the edges of the plastic wrap tightly over the salmon, fit the cardboard on top, then place 2 large cans on the cardboard to weight it. Refrigerate the salmon for 3 days, basting it with its juices once a day.

Once the salmon has cured, remove the weights and the cardboard and unwrap the fish. With a paper towel, wipe off the dill and the salt mixture and pat the fish dry. Refrigerate the salmon uncovered for at least another 6 hours to allow the skin to set.

continued overleaf...

BEET VINAIGRETTE Combine the beet juice, shallots, juniper berries and bay leaf in a small saucepan and cook on medium heat until it is reduced to ¼ cup/60 mL, about 10 minutes. Strain the beet reduction through a fine-mesh sieve into a clean bowl and discard the solids. Add the gin, orange juice, red wine vinegar and olive oil and whisk until emulsified. Season with salt and freshly ground black pepper. Will keep refrigerated in an airtight container for up to 5 days.

NEW POTATOES In a small saucepan, combine the potatoes, tarragon, bay leaf and a large pinch of salt. Bring to a boil on high heat, then reduce the heat to low and allow to simmer until the potatoes are tender, about 20 minutes. Remove from the heat, drain and allow to cool.

Slice the potatoes thinly, then place them in a small bowl and toss with the olive oil.

TO SERVE Using a very sharp knife, thinly slice the salmon diagonally across the fillet and remove and discard the skin. With a pastry brush, paint 2 spoonfuls of vinaigrette onto each plate. Arrange potato slices over the vinaigrette and top with 3 or 4 slices of salmon. Drizzle with crème fraîche and garnish with roasted beets, baby watercress (or salad greens) and caviar (or beet or cucumber pearls).

WINE A Riesling (German Kabinett, or Austrian or Australian versions) or, better yet, a Chardonnay from Argentina or Napa would be contrasting but excellent whites; rosé Champagne would be divine, and New World Pinot Noir (Oregon) is a good red choice.

BEET VINAIGRETTE

1 cup	fresh beet juice	250 mL
1	shallot, minced	1
1 Tbsp	juniper berries	15 mL
1	bay leaf	1
2 Tbsp	gin	30 mL
	Juice of 1 orange	
2 Tbsp	red wine vinegar	30 mL
¾ cup	extra-virgin olive oil	185 mL

NEW POTATOES AND GARNISH

1 cup	new potatoes	240 mL
1 sprig	tarragon	1 sprig
1	bay leaf	1
1 Tbsp	extra-virgin olive oil	15 mL
2 Tbsp	crème fraîche	30 mL
¾ cup	roasted beets (page 116)	180 mL
1 cup	baby watercress or salad greens	240 mL
1 Tbsp	caviar or beet or cucumber pearls (page 159)	15 mL

Albacore Tuna Tataki *with* Baby Vegetables *and* Nasturtiums

Serves 4

TUNA TATAKI

8 oz	boneless, skinless albacore tuna loin	225 g
1 tsp	shichimi togarashi (Japanese seven-spice seasoning)	5 mL
1 tsp	grapeseed oil	5 mL
1 Tbsp	Maldon salt or sea salt	15 mL
¼ cup	ponzu sauce (page 237)	60 mL

BABY VEGETABLES

8	baby carrots	8
8	baby white turnips	8
8	baby golden beets	8
12	baby shiitake mushrooms	12
8	baby zucchinis	8
8	radishes	8
1 tsp	toasted sesame oil	5 mL
1 Tbsp	grapeseed oil	15 mL
1 Tbsp	rice vinegar	15 mL
12	nasturtium leaves	12
4	nasturtium blossoms	4

Simple preparations are the true measure of a great product: the less you do to food, the more it shows. Tataki, which involves briefly searing meat or fish over a very hot flame, is one such preparation. For this dish, I use albacore tuna because it has a richer flavour and softer texture that I find superior to its bright red cousin, yellowfin. The peppery tones of the nasturtiums pair well with the richness of the tuna. Look for shichimi togarashi at Asian food stores and Maldon salt at fine grocers.

TUNA TATAKI Season all sides of the tuna loin with the shichimi. Heat a sauté pan on high heat. When the pan is almost smoking, add grapeseed oil and then the tuna loin. Sear the fish on each side for 30 to 40 seconds. Remove from the pan, transfer to a plate and refrigerate immediately to stop the cooking process. Allow the tuna to cool for 1 hour.

BABY VEGETABLES Peel the carrots, turnips and beets. Cut the stems from the shiitake mushrooms and discard. Using a mandoline or a sharp knife, slice the carrots, turnips, beets, zucchinis and radishes lengthwise, as thinly as possible. Slice the shiitake mushrooms.

Fill a large bowl with ice water. Bring a pot of salted water to a boil on high heat. Add the turnips and beets and blanch for 90 seconds. Use a slotted spoon to transfer them to the ice water to stop the cooking. Add the carrots and mushrooms and cook for 60 seconds, then transfer them to the ice water. Repeat with the zucchini, cooking it for 30 seconds before plunging it into the ice water. The radishes do not need blanching.

Transfer all of the blanched vegetables to a tea towel to drain. Pat them dry. In a bowl, combine the blanched vegetables and the radishes. Add the sesame and grapeseed oils and the rice vinegar and toss well.

TO SERVE Using a very sharp knife, slice the tuna into 12 to 16 slices. Arrange 3 nasturtium leaves on each plate and top with an eighth of the vegetables. Place 3 or 4 slices of tuna atop the vegetables and season with some Maldon (or sea) salt. Top with the remaining vegetables and garnish each plate with a nasturtium blossom and a drizzle of the ponzu sauce.

WINE German Riesling will work well, or have some fun trying different varieties of chilled top-quality sake.

Seafood Ceviche *with* Baby Cucumbers *and* Corn Chips

Serves 6

SEAFOOD CEVICHE

1½ lbs	very fresh seafood, deboned, skin removed, shucked, peeled and thawed	680 g
	Juice of 1 lemon	
	Juice of 2 limes	
	Zest of 1 lime	
4	plum tomatoes, peeled, seeded and finely chopped (about ½ cup/125 mL)	4
1	small red onion, finely minced	1
2	red jalapeño peppers, seeded and finely chopped	2
3 Tbsp	extra-virgin olive oil	45 mL
2 tsp	salt	10 mL
2 Tbsp	chopped fresh cilantro	30 mL
1 Tbsp	chopped fresh parsley	15 mL
6	baby cucumbers, halved lengthwise	6

The folks at Island Scallops in Qualicum Beach have developed a cross between a Pacific and a weathervane scallop that is perfect for this recipe. Scallops are like sponges: they are excellent at soaking up flavours. However, they have a fresh, briny and slightly sweet taste all their own, so the less you do to scallops, the better. Since ceviche is made by marinating raw fish or seafood in citrus juice, use only very fresh seafood in this recipe. A combination of four to five different types, such as salmon, spot prawns, sahimi-grade red tuna, sole and/or scallops works well.

SEAFOOD CEVICHE Fill a large roasting pan with ice. Chop the seafood into ¼-inch/5-mm dice and place in a stainless steel bowl. Set the bowl into the roasting pan. Add the lemon juice, lime juice, lime zest, tomatoes, onions, jalapeño peppers, olive oil and salt to the bowl of seafood and toss until well combined. Cover the ceviche and refrigerate for 4 hours, so it can marinate.

CORN CHIPS Preheat the oven to 350°F/175°C.

Cut each tortilla into 8 pie-shaped wedges. Using a pastry brush, lightly brush the tortillas with olive oil and place them on a baking sheet. Combine the cumin and salt in a small bowl. Season the tortilla wedges liberally with the spicy salt mixture and bake them until crisp, 7 to 8 minutes, turning once. Remove the chips from the oven and allow them to cool and crisp further.

TO SERVE Add the cilantro and parsley to the ceviche and toss gently. Arrange 2 cucumber halves, cut side up, on each plate. Spoon ceviche along the top of each piece of cucumber, then drizzle with some of the marinade. Garnish each serving with 2 to 3 corn chips.

WINE A Vermentino from Sardinia or coastal Tuscany would be a natural seaside match worth seeking out.

CORN CHIPS

4	corn tortillas, each 6 inches/15 cm in diameter	4
1 Tbsp	extra-virgin olive oil	15 mL
1 tsp	ground cumin	5 mL
1 tsp	kosher salt	5 mL

Spot Prawn Salad *with* Cucumber Broth, Cilantro *and* Arugula

Serves 4

ORANGE VINAIGRETTE

¼ cup	freshly squeezed orange juice	60 mL
2 Tbsp	extra-virgin olive oil	30 mL

SPOT PRAWN SALAD

1	lemon	1
3 to 4 Tbsp	kosher salt	45 to 60 mL
33	wild B.C. spot prawns, large size, shells on	33
1 tsp	Maldon salt	5 mL
4 sprigs	fresh cilantro, leaves only	4 sprigs
12 slices	heirloom tomatoes, each ½-inch/ 1-cm thick	12 slices
1 cup	arugula, cut in thin strips	240 mL
1 Tbsp	basil oil (page 235)	15 mL

Spot prawns are considered the jewels of the ocean because of their soft texture and sweet flavour. Although they are available fresh for just six weeks, from May to July, spot prawns freeze well and can be found at fish stores year-round. This dish uses clean flavours to highlight the sweetness of the prawns.

ORANGE VINAIGRETTE In a small pot, cook the orange juice on medium heat until reduced by half, 6 to 8 minutes. You should have 2 Tbsp/30 mL remaining. Remove from the heat and refrigerate until cooled, about 15 minutes. Add olive oil and a pinch of salt and whisk until well combined. Will keep refrigerated in an airtight container for up to 5 days.

SPOT PRAWN SALAD Bring a large pot of water to a boil on high heat. Cut the lemon in half, squeeze as much juice as possible into the water, then drop the lemon halves into the water. Add the kosher salt and stir well. The poaching liquid should taste like the Pacific Ocean.

Reduce the heat to medium. Fill a large bowl with ice water. Drop the spot prawns into the poaching liquid all at once and cook for 2 to 3 minutes. To check for doneness, break a prawn in half: if the middle is firm and no longer translucent, the prawns are done. Drain the prawns using a colander and immediately place them in the ice water to cool. Using a slotted spoon, transfer the prawns to a clean bowl and refrigerate for 30 minutes, until the shellfish are chilled.

Peel the prawns and discard the shells. Toss the prawns with about 1 Tbsp/15 mL of the orange vinaigrette (reserving 3 Tbsp/45 mL for dressing the salad) and sprinkle with the Maldon salt. Set aside.

RED WINE GASTRIQUE In a small pot, stir together the sugar and water. Cook on medium heat, without stirring, until the mixture becomes amber, about 5 minutes. Be careful, as the caramel will be very hot. Remove from the heat, carefully add the red wine vinegar (do not stir), return to the stove and gently heat until the caramel is dissolved, about 5 minutes. Remove the gastrique from the heat and refrigerate until it is chilled, about 30 minutes. Will keep refrigerated in an airtight container for up to 10 days.

CUCUMBER BROTH Place the cucumber in a juicer and process according to the manufacturer's instructions. (If you do not have a juicer, purée the cucumber in a bar blender, then strain the mixture through a fine-mesh sieve and discard the solids.) Pour the cucumber juice into a small bowl, add the gastrique and season with Maldon salt. Will keep refrigerated in an airtight container for 1 day.

TO SERVE Divide the cucumber broth among 4 individual bowls. Sprinkle each serving with cilantro. Place a tomato slice in the bottom of each bowl, then top with 4 spot prawns. Top with a tomato slice. Add one more layer of prawns and final tomato slice. In a small bowl, toss the arugula with the reserved orange vinaigrette. Divide the arugula among the 4 servings, placing it on top of the final tomato layer. Drizzle each salad with a couple of drops of basil oil.

WINE Delicate B.C. Riesling or Gewürztraminer won't overpower the sweet prawns, or choose a crisp, light Chablis.

RED WINE GASTRIQUE

¼ cup	granulated sugar	60 mL
2 Tbsp	water	30 mL
¼ cup	red wine vinegar	60 mL

CUCUMBER BROTH

1	cucumber, seeded	1
1 Tbsp	red wine gastrique	15 mL
	Pinch of Maldon salt	

Scallop Tartare *with* Avocado-Citrus Salad *and* Fried Ginger

Serves 4

SCALLOP TARTARE

12	medium fresh Pacific or weathervane scallops	12
3 Tbsp	extra-virgin olive oil	45 mL
	Juice and zest of 1 lime	
½ tsp	pink peppercorns, crushed	2.5 mL
1	small jalapeño pepper, seeded and minced	1
1	green onion, green part only, minced	1
1	large seedless orange	1
1	ripe avocado	1
1 tsp	Maldon salt or sea salt	5 mL
⅛ cup	micro greens or baby lettuces	30 mL

FRIED GINGER

8 cups	vegetable or peanut oil, for deep-frying	2 L
1-inch piece	fresh ginger, peeled	2.5-cm piece

This is a perfect dish for a hot summer day by the ocean. Don't be in a rush to eat it; let it marinate a few hours to develop the flavours. You can also try making this recipe with salmon or albacore tuna for a different flavour.

SCALLOP TARTARE Using a sharp knife, slice the scallops as thinly as possible to obtain 4 to 5 slices from each one. Place the scallops in a stainless steel bowl, then add the olive oil, lime juice, lime zest, pink peppercorns, jalapeño peppers and green onions. Toss gently to combine and refrigerate for 1 to 2 hours, or until well chilled.

Peel the orange and discard the rind. With a paring knife, remove and discard the skin and pith from each segment. Set aside the orange segments. Halve the avocado lengthwise and discard the pit. Cut each half in half again lengthwise, then slide a knife just under the skin of each segment and peel it off. Discard the avocado skins. Thinly slice the avocado along its length and set aside.

FRIED GINGER Fill a deep pot or a wok two-thirds full with vegetable (or peanut) oil and heat it to 330°F/165°C (use a deep-fat thermometer to check the temperature).

Using a very sharp knife, slice the ginger as thinly as possible. Place the ginger in a colander and set it under cold running water for 10 minutes. Rinsing the ginger removes its harsh flavour. Pat the ginger dry with a tea towel. Deep-fry the ginger until crisp and golden, about 3 minutes, then remove from the oil and drain on paper towels.

TO SERVE Sprinkle the scallops with the Maldon (or sea) salt and toss gently. Arrange a quarter of the avocado slices on each plate. Top with alternating layers of scallops and orange segments until you have 3 layers altogether. Spoon some of the scallop marinade over each serving and garnish with micro greens (or baby lettuces) and fried ginger.

WINE Opt for a good-quality Mosel Riesling (Kabinett) or an Italian Fiano di Avellino.

Heirloom Tomato Salad *with* Buffalo Mozzarella

Serves 4

Underripe or watery tomatoes are so flavourless and mealy that there should be a law against serving them. Make this salad only with ripe, juicy fruit that has been harvested locally. Any heirloom variety will work, though I particularly like Brandywine and Oxheart ones from the Okanagan Valley. Substitute arugula for the lettuces and Parmesan cheese for the mozzarella, if you prefer.

TOMATO CHIPS If you have one, use a food dehydrator to make these tomato chips. To make them in the oven, preheat the oven to 100°F/40°C or lower. Line a baking sheet with parchment paper and brush it lightly with olive oil.

Slice the tomatoes as thinly as possible and place them on the baking sheet. Bake the tomatoes for 6 to 8 hours, placing a damp, balled-up towel in the oven door to keep it slightly ajar.

HEIRLOOM TOMATO SALAD In a stainless steel bowl, combine the tomatoes, lemon thyme, olive oil and sherry vinegar and season with half the salt.

TO SERVE Arrange a quarter of the lollo rosso and oak leaf lettuce leaves on each plate. Season the mozzarella with the remaining Maldon (or sea) salt. Place a slice of mozzarella on each bed of lettuce, then top with an eighth of the tomato mixture. Repeat with another layer of mozzarella and tomatoes. Spoon some of the marinade from the tomatoes over each dish and garnish with a few tomato chips.

WINE I love to pair this dish with a Spanish white from Rueda, such as Telmo Rodriguez's Basa, or Greco di Tufo from Campania, Italy.

TOMATO CHIPS

1 tsp	olive oil for brushing	5 mL
3	ripe but firm tomatoes	3

HEIRLOOM TOMATO SALAD

1 lb	mixed heirloom or assorted ripe, tomatoes sliced	455 g
1 tsp	lemon thyme leaves	5 mL
3 Tbsp	extra-virgin olive oil	45 mL
2 Tbsp	sherry vinegar	30 mL
1 head	lollo rosso lettuce, washed and trimmed	1 head
1 head	oak leaf lettuce, washed and trimmed	1 head
8 oz	buffalo mozzarella, cut in 8 slices	225 g
1 tsp	Maldon salt or sea salt	5 mL
2 sprigs	fresh basil	2 sprigs

Roasted Lingcod *with* Saffron Potatoes *and* White Asparagus

Serves 4

SAFFRON POTATOES

1 ⅛ lbs	new potatoes, peeled and left whole	500 g
6 cups	vegetable stock (page 233)	1.5 L
½ tsp	saffron threads	5 mL
1	dried bay leaf (or 2 fresh)	1
2 Tbsp	unsalted butter	30 mL
1 Tbsp	chopped fresh parsley	15 mL

WHITE ASPARAGUS

2 cups	vegetable stock (page 233)	500 mL
1 Tbsp	granulated sugar	15 mL
1 sprig	fresh thyme	1 sprig
1 tsp	kosher salt	5 mL
16 spears	white asparagus, trimmed and well peeled	16 spears
1 Tbsp	butter	15 mL

Saffron may seem like an expensive ingredient to be using with potatoes, but Pemberton potatoes are well worth it. Don't be afraid to cook the white asparagus for a long time; the spears are not as delicate as the green ones. Lingcod are incredibly moist and their flesh is quite firm, which makes it suitable for many applications.

SAFFRON POTATOES Place the potatoes, vegetable stock, saffron and bay leaf (or leaves) in a medium saucepan and add a healthy pinch of salt. Bring to a boil on high heat, then reduce the heat to medium and simmer until the potatoes are tender when pierced with a knife, 20 to 25 minutes. Drain the potatoes, reserving the saffron cooking liquid to make soup bases or to cook rice (will keep refrigerated in an airtight container for 3 days or frozen for a month). Allow the potatoes to cool to room temperature.

WHITE ASPARAGUS Heat the vegetable stock in a medium saucepan on high heat, then add the sugar, thyme, salt and asparagus. Reduce the heat to medium and simmer for 15 to 20 minutes, until the asparagus spears are very tender when pierced with a knife. Remove the saucepan from the heat and allow the asparagus to cool in the cooking juices.

ROASTED LINGCOD Preheat the oven to 400°F/205°C. In an ovenproof sauté pan, heat the clarified butter on medium heat. Season the lingcod with kosher salt, then arrange the fillets skin side down in the pan. Add the garlic and tarragon. Place the pan in the oven and roast for 8 to 10 minutes, until the fish is firm to the touch.

TO SERVE Place the white asparagus, butter and a couple of spoonfuls of the asparagus's cooking liquid in a sauté pan on medium heat and warm through. Heat the potatoes and butter in a medium saucepan on medium heat and warm through. Sprinkle with the parsley. Remove the lingcod fillets from the oven and turn them flesh side down. Lightly baste the skin with the pan juices, then transfer to a paper towel to drain. Divide the asparagus among 4 plates, then top with a quarter of the saffron potatoes. Place a lingcod fillet on the potatoes and spoon lemon vinaigrette over the fish.

WINE Pair this dish with grand cru Chablis, Condrieu or a California white Rhône blend, like the one from Treana Winery.

ROASTED LINGCOD

2 Tbsp	clarified butter (page 232)	30 mL
4 fillets	fresh lingcod, each 6 oz/170 g, skin on and bones removed	4 fillets
½ tsp	kosher salt	2.5 mL
3 cloves	garlic, halved	3 cloves
2 sprigs	fresh tarragon	2 sprigs
6 Tbsp	lemon vinaigrette (page 30)	90 mL

Wild Salmon *with* Artichoke *and* Vegetable Medley

Serves 4

ARTICHOKE AND VEGETABLE MEDLEY

1 ¾ cups	water	435 mL
1 ¾ cups	dry white wine	435 mL
3 ½ cups	vegetable or chicken stock (pages 233, 235)	875 mL
	Juice of 2 lemons	
6	large fresh globe artichokes	6
1 cup	extra-virgin olive oil	250 mL
1	small onion, chopped in ¼-inch/5-mm cubes	1
1 cup	sliced carrots	240 mL
1	small bulb fennel, halved, core removed and thinly sliced	1
2	shallots, sliced into rings	2
1 clove	garlic, minced	1 clove
2 tsp	kosher salt	10 mL
1	bay leaf	1
1 sprig	fresh thyme	1 sprig
2 sprigs	fresh parsley	2 sprigs
2 cups	green beans, cooked for 4 minutes in salted water, refreshed in cold water and drained	480 mL
½ recipe	ricotta gnocchi, cooked, refreshed in cold water and drained (page 74)	½ recipe
2 Tbsp	butter, cold	30 mL

The great thing about salmon is that there are so many different types available. Spring salmon (also known as chinook) works well here due to its richness, which is nicely cut by the tangy broth. Try this recipe with other varieties of salmon throughout the season. When buying artichokes, look for ones that are deep green, heavy for their size and have a tight leaf formation.

ARTICHOKE AND VEGETABLE MEDLEY Combine water, white wine, vegetable (or chicken) stock and lemon juice in a large bowl.

With scissors or a sharp knife, cut off the top third of the artichoke leaves. Remove and discard the tough outer leaves, stopping only when you reach the softer light green leaves. With a potato peeler or a paring knife, peel the stalk and the base of each artichoke. Place the artichokes in the stock mixture to soften them and prevent them from discolouring.

Using a large saucepan fitted with a lid, heat the olive oil on medium heat, then add onions, carrots, fennel and shallots and sauté for 5 to 6 minutes to soften. Remove the artichokes from the stock mixture and add them to the sautéed vegetables. Reserve the stock mixture. Stir the garlic into the vegetables, add the kosher salt, cover the pot and cook for 10 minutes. Increase the heat to high. Pour the stock mixture over the vegetables, add the bay leaf and the thyme and parsley sprigs, and bring to a boil, uncovered. Reduce the heat to low, cover the pot again and simmer gently for 10 minutes, or until the artichokes are tender. A knife or skewer inserted into the base should come out easily. Remove the vegetables from the heat.

continued overleaf…

2 Tbsp	clarified butter (page 232)	30 mL
4 fillets	fresh wild spring (chinook or king) salmon, each 5 oz/140 g, skin on but bones removed	4 fillets
	Juice of 1 lemon	

Using a slotted spoon, transfer the artichokes to a medium bowl and refrigerate them for 30 minutes, until chilled. Remove and discard the bay leaf and the thyme and parsley sprigs. Reserve the vegetables and the broth.

To finish the artichokes, cut them in half lengthwise and use a spoon to scoop out and discard the chokes. Remove and discard any leaves that are not as tender as you would like. Cut the artichoke halves in half lengthwise once more, add them to the vegetables and broth and bring to a gentle simmer on low heat.

BAKED SALMON Preheat the oven to 400°F/205°C. Heat the butter in an ovenproof sauté pan on medium heat. Season the salmon fillets with salt, then fry them, skin side down, for 2 minutes. Place the pan in the oven for 6 to 7 minutes more, or until the flesh is firm to the touch. Remove from the oven.

Turn the salmon fillets over. Drizzle the flesh side with lemon juice, then spoon the pan juices over the fillets.

TO SERVE Add the green beans and the gnocchi to the vegetable medley to warm them through, about 3 minutes, then stir in the cold butter to enrich the broth. Divide the vegetables and broth among four bowls and top each serving with a salmon fillet.

WINE B.C. Chenin Blanc, New Zealand Sauvignon Blanc or a modern Greek white will hold up to the artichokes; southern French rosé or lighter Loire red or B.C. Cabernet Franc may match well also.

Prosciutto-wrapped Halibut
with Littleneck Clam Chowder

Serves 4

I always like to serve halibut either wrapped or crusted, probably because it is a firm fish with a light flavour. In this dish, the crisp prosciutto seals in the natural juices of the fish. Buy the prosciutto very thinly sliced for best results.

PROSCIUTTO-WRAPPED HALIBUT Arrange the prosciutto slices on a clean work surface. Place a sage leaf on each one. Position a halibut fillet along the shorter bottom edge of each slice. Fold the bottom of the prosciutto over the fish and tightly roll the halibut in the prosciutto until you have four log-shaped packages. Wrap each package tightly in plastic wrap and refrigerate for 30 minutes, until chilled.

CLAMS Using a large saucepan fitted with a lid, heat the olive oil on medium heat. Add the shallots and sauté until softened, about 3 minutes. Increase the heat to high and add the clams, white wine, fish stock and thyme sprig, then cover. After 2 minutes, use a slotted spoon to transfer any open clams to a small bowl. Continue to remove the clams as they open; discard any clams that have not opened after 5 minutes. Remove the broth from the heat, strain through a fine-mesh sieve and reserve for the chowder. Remove the clam meat from the shells and reserve. Discard the shells.

continued overleaf...

PROSCIUTTO-WRAPPED HALIBUT

4 slices	prosciutto, each 2 × 6 inches/ 5 × 15 cm	4 slices
4	large sage leaves	4
4 fillets	fresh halibut, each 5 oz/140 g, skin removed	4 fillets
2 Tbsp	olive oil	30 mL

CLAMS

1 Tbsp	olive oil	15 mL
2	shallots, sliced	2
1 lb	littleneck clams, rinsed and shells closed	455 g
¼ cup	white wine	60 mL
¼ cup	fish stock (page 233)	60 mL
1 sprig	fresh thyme	1 sprig

CLAM CHOWDER In a medium saucepan on low heat, gently heat the clam broth, fish stock, milk and bay leaf.

Melt the butter in a second medium saucepan on medium heat. Slowly add the flour, whisking gently to form a roux. Reduce the heat to low and cook for 5 minutes. Whisk in the hot broth-milk mixture, slowly at first to avoid lumps. Gently simmer this velouté sauce for 10 minutes, then stir in the cream. Strain the sauce through a fine-mesh sieve and set aside.

Heat the grapeseed oil in a medium saucepan on medium heat. Add the bacon and sauté until lightly crisped, about 5 minutes. Add the potatoes, leeks and carrots and sauté on medium heat for 3 to 4 minutes. Pour off any excess oil, then stir in the celery and the velouté sauce and simmer until the potatoes are tender, 8 to 10 minutes. Add the reserved clams to warm them through.

FINISH HALIBUT Preheat the oven to 375°F/190°C and remove the halibut logs from the plastic wrap. Heat the olive oil in an ovenproof sauté pan on medium heat. Add the halibut, turning the fillets in the pan to lightly crisp the prosciutto on each side, for about 3 minutes in total. Place the pan in the oven and bake for 4 to 5 minutes more, or until the halibut is firm to the touch. Transfer the fillets to a clean cutting surface and slice each one into three pieces.

TO SERVE Add the parsley to the chowder. Ladle the chowder into 4 individual bowls, then top each serving with 3 pieces of the prosciutto-wrapped halibut. Serve immediately.

WINE This dish is very white wine–friendly but deserves fine white Burgundy, Austrian Grüner Veltliner or Riesling, or the best B.C. Chardonnay or Pinot Blanc available.

CLAM CHOWDER

1 cup	clam broth	250 mL
2 cups	fish stock (page 233)	500 mL
1 cup	whole milk	250 mL
1	bay leaf	1
¼ cup	unsalted butter	60 mL
¼ cup	all-purpose, flour sifted	60 mL
¼ cup	whipping cream	60 mL
1 Tbsp	grapeseed oil	15 mL
2 slices	bacon, diced	2 slices
1	large Yukon Gold or Désirée potato, peeled and diced	1
1	medium leek, white and light green parts only, sliced and rinsed	1
1	medium carrot, diced	1
2 stalks	celery, diced	2 stalks
	reserved clam meat	
1 Tbsp	chopped fresh parsley	15 mL

Seared Red Tuna *with* Chickpea Panisse *and* Salsa Verde

Serves 4

SALSA VERDE

1 slice	white bread, crusts removed, cut in 6 to 8 pieces	1 slice
2 Tbsp	white wine vinegar	30 mL
3 Tbsp	capers, rinsed and chopped	45 mL
1 cup	mixed herbs (mint, tarragon, basil, parsley)	240 mL
1 tsp	granulated sugar	5 mL
2 Tbsp	extra-virgin olive oil	30 mL

CHICKPEA PANISSE

¼ cup	olive oil	60 mL
½	small onion, minced	½
1 tsp	curry powder	5 mL
1 clove	garlic, minced	1 clove
6 cups	chicken or vegetable stock (pages 235, 233)	1.5 L
1½ cups	chickpea flour, sifted	355 mL
	Juice of 1 lemon	
¼ cup	grated Parmesan cheese	60 mL

This dish brings together some of the flavours of summer—and provides a good way to use up some of that bounty when it threatens to overwhelm you. When your herbs are taking over the garden, use the leaves in salads or make this tangy salsa verde to accompany the tender young beans that are one of the highlights of the summer. Sashimi-grade yellowfin tuna is often referred to as red tuna; it is what we use in this recipe. At the restaurant we serve this dish with panisse, a creamy rich cake made from chickpea flour that's popular in the south of France, which we cut and fry as an alternative to French fries.

SALSA VERDE Place all of the ingredients in a food processor or a blender and process until you obtain a beautiful uniform green paste. Be careful not to process the salsa for too long or it will lose its freshness. If the salsa is too thick, add a little ice water. Transfer the salsa to a stainless steel bowl and refrigerate until chilled, about 30 minutes. Will keep refrigerated in an airtight container for up to 2 days.

CHICKPEA PANISSE Lightly grease a 9 × 11-inch/ 22.5 × 30-cm cake pan.

Heat 2 Tbsp/30 mL of the olive oil in a medium saucepan on medium heat. Add the onions and sauté until softened, 4 to 5 minutes. Stir in the curry powder and garlic and sauté for 4 to 5 minutes more. Pour in the chicken (or vegetable) stock and bring it to a simmer. Reduce the heat to medium-low, then slowly add the chickpea flour, whisking constantly and forcefully (some lumps will develop but just keep whisking), and cook for 8 to 10 minutes, until the panisse batter has a smooth consistency.

Stir in the lemon juice and season generously with salt and pepper. Finish with the Parmesan cheese. Remove the batter from the heat and pour it into the prepared cake pan. Refrigerate until chilled, about 1 hour.

Using a sharp knife or a round cutter, cut the panisse into 3-inch/7.5-cm rounds (or to any size you prefer). Heat the remaining 2 Tbsp/30 mL of olive oil in a non-stick sauté pan on medium-low heat. Add the panisse rounds and cook until golden brown, 2 to 3 minutes per side, depending on the thickness. Transfer the panisse to a large plate and reserve the sauté pan, pouring off any excess oil.

TUNA Place the reserved sauté pan on high heat. Brush the tuna with olive oil and liberally season it with black pepper and kosher salt. Place the tuna into the hot pan and sear on each side for 30 to 45 seconds to crisp the pepper. Remove from the pan and cut into ½-inch/1-cm slices.

In a small bowl, toss the beans with one-third of the salsa verde. Season lightly with kosher salt.

TO SERVE Arrange a quarter of the green beans on each plate. Place a panisse disc over the beans and top the panisse with a portion of tuna. Drizzle with the remaining salsa verde and serve immediately.

WINE A medium-bodied Mediterranean red (think south of France), Dolcetto or Oregon Pinot Noir would be best.

TUNA

1¼ lbs	sashimi-grade yellowfin tuna, in 4 portions	560 g
1 Tbsp	olive oil	15 mL
1 tsp	cracked black pepper	5 mL
½ tsp	kosher salt	2.5 mL
1 cup	baby green beans, blanched	240 mL

Herb-crusted Halibut *with* Pea Purée *and* Coriander Vinaigrette

Serves 4

HERB-CRUSTED HALIBUT

1½ oz	fresh herb leaves (such as basil, parsley, chervil or tarragon), about ¾ cup/180 mL	40 g
1 oz	spinach, washed and trimmed, about ½ cup/120 mL	30 g
1 cup	grated Gruyère cheese	240 mL
½ cup	unsalted butter, softened	120 mL
1¾ cups	dry bread crumbs	420 mL
4 fillets	fresh halibut, each 5 to 6 oz/140 to 170 g, skin on but bones removed	4 fillets
2 tsp	olive oil	10 mL

To me, this dish combines all the flavours of summer on one plate. The crust in this recipe can be used to coat meats, poultry or vegetables. Experiment with different herbs and greens, such as arugula or sorrel leaves.

HERB-CRUSTED HALIBUT Place the herbs and the spinach in a food processor and purée for 1 to 2 minutes. Scrape down the sides of the bowl, then add the Gruyère cheese and the butter and purée until well combined. Pour in the bread crumbs, lightly season with salt and process until the mixture comes together.

Cut two 11 × 16-inch/30 × 40-cm sheets of parchment paper and place 1 on a baking sheet. Spread the bread crumb mixture onto the parchment paper, cover with the second sheet, then use a rolling pin to roll the bread crumb mixture to a thickness of ⅛ inch/3 mm. Place the baking sheet in the refrigerator for 30 minutes to allow the crust to set.

Cut the crust into 4 pieces, each one large enough to cover one side of one fillet. Return these cut pieces to the refrigerator.

continued overleaf...

PEA PURÉE Heat half of the butter in a small saucepan on medium heat. Add the onions and the bacon and sauté until lightly golden, about 5 minutes. Stir in half of the peas and the chicken stock, potato, mint and thyme and bring to a boil. Simmer gently until the potato is tender, about 8 minutes. Remove and discard the mint and thyme sprigs. Add the remaining peas and cook for 3 minutes more. Remove from the heat, lightly season with salt and pepper, then transfer to a food processor or a blender and purée until smooth. Stir in the cream and set aside.

CORIANDER VINAIGRETTE Crush the coriander seeds using a mortar and pestle, then place them in a sauté pan and warm them gently on low heat to release their flavour.

In a small bowl, whisk together the olive oil and lemon juice, then add the coriander and a pinch of salt. Set aside.

FINISH HALIBUT Preheat the oven to 375°F/190°C. Lightly oil a baking sheet.

Arrange the halibut on the baking sheet. Lightly season with salt, then place a herb crust atop each fillet. Bake for 9 to 11 minutes, until the crust is crisp and the halibut is slightly opaque in the middle. Remove from the oven.

TO SERVE Warm the vinaigrette in a saucepan on low heat. Add the tomatoes and the asparagus and heat through. Divide the pea purée among the 4 plates, mounding it in the centre of each plate. Top each serving with a halibut fillet, then spoon a generous amount of vinaigrette around each plate. Garnish with the oregano leaves.

WINE New Zealand Sauvignon Blanc, Sancerre, Pouilly-Fumé, B.C. or Washington Sémillon, or Grüner Veltliner would be an excellent choice.

PEA PURÉE

¼ cup	unsalted butter	60 mL
1	small white onion, finely chopped	1
2 oz	bacon, about 4 to 5 slices, cut in small dice	60 g
1 cup	fresh shucked peas or thawed frozen peas	240 mL
⅔ cup	chicken stock (page 235)	165 mL
1	medium potato, peeled and cut in small dice	1
1 sprig	mint	1 sprig
1 sprig	thyme	1 sprig
2 Tbsp	whipping cream	30 mL

CORIANDER VINAIGRETTE

2 tsp	coriander seeds	10 mL
1 cup	olive oil	250 mL
⅓ cup	fresh lemon juice	80 mL
3	Roma tomatoes, peeled, seeded and cut in ¼-inch/5-mm dice	3
16	asparagus tips, blanched for 2 minutes and refreshed in cold water	16
2 tsp	oregano leaves, for garnish	2 tsp

Seafood Boudin *with* Caponata

Serves 4 to 6 (Yields twelve 4-inch/10-cm sausages)

SEAFOOD BOUDIN

5	egg whites	5
4 to 5 slices	white bread, crusts removed	4 to 5 slices
1⅔ cups	whipping cream	415 mL
1½ lbs	fresh cod or sole, skin and bones removed	680 g
¼ cup	crushed ice	60 mL
2 Tbsp	brandy	30 mL
½ tsp	cayenne pepper	2.5 mL
1½ Tbsp	kosher salt	25 mL
2 Tbsp	lemon juice	30 mL
6 oz	scallops, cut in ⅛-inch/3-mm dice	170 g
6 oz	spot prawns, cut in ⅛-inch/3-mm dice	170 g
1 Tbsp	chopped fresh tarragon	15 mL
1 Tbsp	chopped fresh chervil	15 mL
3 ft	hog casing, rinsed inside and out with cold water	1 m
13 pieces	kitchen string, in 3-inch/7.5-cm lengths	13 pieces
2 Tbsp	grapeseed oil	30 mL

A boudin is a sausage, and anyone interested in cooking should make sausages at least a few times. Although they are time consuming to make, homemade sausages provide not only a great sense of accomplishment when you eat the finished product but they taste better for the experience. Caponata is a Sicilian dish made from eggplants that is served at room temperature and used as a salad, side dish or relish. The sweet and sour flavours in the caponata complement the sausage and work well with grilled meats too. Serve a light salad of mixed greens as an accompaniment to this dish.

SEAFOOD BOUDIN In a medium bowl, combine the egg whites, bread and ½ cup/125 mL of the cream. Refrigerate for 30 minutes until well chilled.

Place the cod (or sole) and the ice in a food processor and purée at high speed for 1 minute. Scrape down the sides and add the bread mixture. Process at high speed for another 2 minutes while adding half of the remaining cream. Transfer this fish mixture to a medium bowl and refrigerate for 30 minutes.

Press the fish mixture through a fine-mesh sieve, discarding any solids, then refrigerate for another 30 minutes until well chilled. Gently fold in the remaining cream and the brandy, cayenne, salt and lemon juice, then add the scallops, prawns, tarragon and chervil and mix lightly. (You can check the seasoning by poaching or lightly sautéing a small amount of the mixture to determine how it will taste when cooked.) Spoon the seafood mixture into a large piping bag fitted with a large circular tip.

continued overleaf . . .

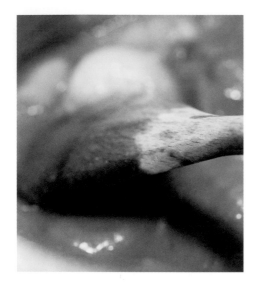

To make the boudin, open one end of the casing and feed all of the casing on to the tip of the piping bag. Be gentle, as the casing is delicate and may tear easily. Tie a tight knot in the second end. Squeeze the piping bag to fill the casing, carefully slipping the filled portions of casing off the tip of the piping bag. Try to fill all of it evenly and avoid air pockets. Once you have piped all the filling into the casing, you will have one big long sausage.

To make individual links, start at the knotted end and measure off 4 inches/10 cm. Slowly and gently pinch the casing where you want to make a link and twist it clockwise. Measure off another 4-inch/10-cm length, then slowly and gently pinch the casing and twist the link counterclockwise. Repeat this process, alternating clockwise and counterclockwise twists with each new link, until you have reached the end of the casing. Secure the sausages by knotting a piece of kitchen string at either end of the casing and between each link.

Fill a large bowl with ice water. Bring a large pot of water to a gentle simmer on medium heat. Use a thermometer to test the water temperature. To cook the sausages, the water temperature should be about 165°F/75°C. Without separating the links, cook the sausages for 9 minutes. To check that they are cooked, cut one open and use the thermometer to take the sausage's internal temperature: it should be 140°F/60°C. Place the sausages in the ice water to stop the cooking, then transfer them to an airtight container and refrigerate. Will keep refrigerated in an airtight container for up to 2 days.

CAPONATA Heat the olive oil in a sauté pan on medium heat. Add the eggplant and sauté until lightly golden brown, about 10 minutes. Stir in the celery and bell peppers and sauté until softened, about 5 minutes. Drain the vegetables on paper towels, then place them in a small bowl. Add the red wine gastrique, pine nuts and raisins. Mix well and set aside.

FINISH SAUSAGES Using scissors, cut the boudin into individual links. With a sharp knife, make a small incision in each link's casing and peel it off and discard. Heat the grapeseed oil in a non-stick pan on low heat. Add the sausages, gently turning them to heat them through. Increase the heat to medium-high to lightly brown the sausages. Drain the sausages on paper towels.

TO SERVE Arrange 3 sausages on each plate and top with a quarter of the caponata.

WINE Sip a Sicilian white or a lighter Italian red, or, at brunch, serve demi-sec Champagne or rosé Prosecco.

CAPONATA

2 Tbsp	olive oil	30 mL
¼ cup	peeled and diced eggplant	60 mL
¼ cup	diced celery	60 mL
¼ cup	seeded and diced red bell pepper	60 mL
2 Tbsp	red wine gastrique (page 45)	30 mL
1 Tbsp	pine nuts, toasted	15 mL
2 Tbsp	sultana raisins, soaked in water and drained	30 mL

Spot Prawn Tortelloni *with* English Peas *and* Lemon Thyme

Serves 4 (Yields about 24 tortelloni)

Filled pastas like these tortelloni—which means "little twist" in Italian—are very easy to make, especially with a little practice. In this dish, the subtle flavours of the prawns in the filling and the peas in the sauce go together very well. Remember to taste some of the peas before you buy or pick them to be sure they are perfect.

PRAWN TORTELLONI Chill the bowl of a food processor and a stainless steel bowl in the refrigerator for 30 minutes. Place the spot prawns and salmon in the food processor bowl and pulse until the seafood is chopped and well combined. Add the salt, nutmeg, lemon juice and lemon zest and pulse again to combine. Add the egg and process at high speed until well mixed, about 2 minutes. Transfer the mixture to the chilled stainless steel bowl and fold in the brandy, followed by the cream and the dill. Refrigerate the prawn filling while you roll out the pasta.

Lightly moisten a tea towel with cold water. Following the instructions on your pasta machine, roll the dough into a sheet the thickness of a dime. Using a round cutter or a glass, cut the dough into twenty-four 3½- to 4-inch/ 9- to 10-cm rounds. Assemble the rounds in a stack and cover them with the damp cloth.

Lightly dust a baking sheet with flour and fill a small bowl with water. Fill a large roasting pan with ice. Place the bowl of prawn filling on the ice while you work with the dough.

continued overleaf...

PRAWN TORTELLONI

1 lb	spot prawns, peeled and shells reserved for sauce, well chilled	455 g
4 oz	wild salmon, skin and bones removed, well chilled	115 g
1½ tsp	kosher salt	7.5 mL
¼ tsp	freshly grated nutmeg	1 mL
	Juice and zest of 1 lemon	
1	egg	1
1 Tbsp	brandy	15 mL
3 Tbsp	whipping cream	45 mL
1 tsp	chopped fresh dill	5 mL
1 recipe	fresh pasta dough (page 241)	1 recipe
1 Tbsp	olive oil	15 mL

2	shallots, minced	2
1 Tbsp	unsalted butter	15 mL
6 Tbsp	vermouth	90 mL
	reserved prawn shells	
1 cup	fish stock (page 233)	250 mL
3 sprigs	lemon thyme	3 sprigs
¾ cup	whipping cream	185 mL
¾ cup	shucked fresh peas, 4 whole pods reserved	180 mL
¼ cup	grated pecorino Romano cheese	60 mL

Place one pasta round on a clean work surface. Spoon 2 tsp/10 mL of the filling onto the centre of the pasta, then, using a pastry brush, lightly brush the edges of the round with water. Fold the top half of the pasta round over the bottom half to form a semi-circle, being careful to completely enclose the filling.

To shape the tortelloni, lay a pasta semi-circle—flat edge toward you—across the middle of your index finger. There should be an even amount of pasta on both sides of your finger. Dab a small amount of water on one corner of the semi-circle, then fold the pasta around your finger, bringing the two tips together. With the thumb and forefinger of your other hand, press the tips together tightly to seal the tortelloni, then carefully slide it off your finger. Place this tortelloni on the baking sheet, and continue filling and shaping the remaining tortelloni until you have used up all the pasta and the filling. Reserve the pasta while you prepare the sauce. Will keep refrigerated, covered with plastic wrap, for 1 day.

LEMON THYME SAUCE AND PEAS Place the shallots and butter in a small saucepan on low heat and sauté until softened but not coloured, about 5 minutes. Increase the heat to medium, add the vermouth and reduce until almost all the liquid has evaporated, about 8 minutes. Add the prawn shells and cook for 5 minutes, or until the shells redden from the heat. Reduce the heat to medium-low, stir in the fish stock and 1 sprig of lemon thyme and simmer until the liquid is reduced by half, about 10 minutes. Pour in the cream, remove from the heat and cover the pot with a lid or plastic wrap. Allow the sauce to infuse for 30 minutes.

Strain the sauce through a fine-mesh sieve into a clean saucepan and discard the solids. Bring the sauce to a simmer on medium heat and add the shucked peas. Cook for 3 minutes, then remove from the heat.

FINISH PRAWN TORTELLONI Bring a large pot of water to a boil on high heat. Add about 1 tsp/5 mL of salt per 4 cups/ 1 L of water. Add the tortelloni and cook for 3 to 4 minutes. To check for doneness, cut a tortelloni in half and look to see if the edges of the dough are cooked. Using a slotted spoon, transfer the tortelloni to a bowl and drizzle with the olive oil.

TO SERVE Place 5 or 6 tortelloni in each bowl and cover with sauce. Split open the whole pea pods to expose the peas and arrange a pod on each serving. Sprinkle each serving with pecorino Romano cheese and lemon thyme leaves. Serve immediately.

WINE There are lots of fun pairing possibilities with this dish, from Italian whites, like top-quality Soave or Falanghina, to Alsace or B.C. Riesling and Pinot Blanc.

Cheese Cannelloni *with* Baby Spinach *and* Tomato Sauce

Serves 4

CANNELLONI

8 oz	soft goat cheese	225 g
⅔ cup	grated pecorino Romano cheese	160 mL
½ cup	ricotta cheese, strained overnight to remove moisture	120 mL
1 Tbsp	chopped chives	15 mL
1 pinch	freshly grated nutmeg	1 pinch
1 tsp	kosher salt	5 mL
½ cup	cooked, riced potato (about 2 medium potatoes)	120 mL
1 recipe	fresh pasta dough (page 241)	1 recipe
4 slices	buffalo mozzarella, each 1½ to 2 oz/ 40 to 60 g	4 slices

When you make cannelloni, make a lot; there is something therapeutic about the preparation process and you can freeze it for rainy days. It's not written in the recipe, but I'd recommend drizzling basil oil (page 235) or olive oil over the finished dish.

CANNELLONI In a large bowl, combine the three cheeses with the chives, nutmeg, salt and potato and blend until well mixed. Spoon this cheese filling into a piping bag fitted with a wide nozzle and set aside at room temperature.

Divide the pasta dough into 4 equal portions. Lightly moisten a tea towel with cold water. Following the instructions on your pasta machine, roll each portion of dough into a sheet with the thickness of a quarter. Trim the pasta sheets so they are about 12 inches/30 cm wide. Assemble the sheets in a stack and cover them with the damp cloth.

Bring a large pot of salted water to a boil on high heat. Add the pasta sheets and cook for 2 minutes. Drain the pasta and place it under cold running water to stop the cooking process. Transfer the cooked pasta to a tea towel and pat it dry. Set aside.

TOMATO SAUCE Place the olive oil, garlic and onion in a medium saucepan on medium-low heat and sauté for 8 to 10 minutes, until softened. Stir in the tomatoes, basil, tomato paste, salt and sugar, then reduce the heat to low and simmer for 15 to 20 minutes. Remove from the heat and discard the basil. Transfer the sauce to a food processor or a blender and purée until smooth, then strain it through a medium-mesh sieve into a clean bowl, discarding any solids. Set aside.

SPINACH Heat a sauté pan on medium heat and add the butter. When it has melted, add the shallots and sauté until lightly golden, about 5 minutes. Stir in the spinach, lightly season it with salt and toss it to coat with butter, then sauté until the spinach is mostly wilted, about 3 minutes. Using tongs, transfer the spinach to a tea towel to drain. Set aside.

TO ASSEMBLE Preheat the oven to 350°F/175°C. Ladle two-thirds of the tomato sauce into the bottom of an ovenproof baking dish or, preferably, divide it among 4 individual gratin dishes. Spread the sauce liberally over the bottom and insides of the dish(es).

Lay out the pasta sheets across a dry work surface. Pipe a quarter of the filling in a line across the edge closest to you. Fold the edge of the pasta sheet over the filling, then fold the pasta sheet and filling over once more to form a log. Trim and discard any excess pasta, then cut each log into three equal pieces. Arrange these cannelloni on the tomato sauce (use 3 per gratin dish), placing a little spinach between each piece. Top the cannelloni with the remaining tomato sauce and a slice of mozzarella per serving. Bake for 15 to 20 minutes, or until the cannelloni are golden brown and bubbling at the edges.

TO SERVE Arrange 3 cannelloni (or a gratin dish) on each plate and serve immediately.

WINE A simple Chianti or good-value red Tuscan IGT will do well, as will a lighter Barbera or Valpolicella.

TOMATO SAUCE

⅓ cup	olive oil	80 mL
1 clove	garlic, sliced	1 clove
½	small onion, sliced	½
28 fl oz	good-quality canned tomatoes, crushed (1 tin)	825 mL
1 sprig	fresh basil	1 sprig
2 Tbsp	tomato paste	30 mL
2 tsp	kosher salt	10 mL
1 tsp	granulated sugar	5 mL

SPINACH

1 Tbsp	unsalted butter	15 mL
1	shallot, minced	1
2 cups	baby spinach, washed and trimmed	480 mL

Ricotta Gnocchi *with* Toasted Hazelnuts *and* Sage

Serves 4 to 6 (Yields about 50 gnocchi)

1 ⅛ lbs	ricotta cheese, strained overnight to remove moisture	500 g
1	large egg	1
1 ½ tsp	kosher salt	7.5 mL
¼ tsp	freshly grated nutmeg	1 mL
1 cup	all-purpose flour	240 mL
1 cup	vegetable nage (page 233)	250 mL
2 Tbsp	butter, cold	30 mL
1 Tbsp	chopped chives	15 mL
¾ cup	hazelnuts, toasted	180 mL
¼ cup	grated pecorino Romano cheese	60 mL
20	dried sage leaves	20

The hazelnuts we have in British Columbia are almond shaped and have a pronounced nutty flavour, and I make this gnocchi with them in mind. Making gnocchi is really easy and they freeze well. Try a touch of hazelnut oil in the dough for even more of a nutty flavour.

COMBINE THE RICOTTA, egg, salt and nutmeg in a large bowl and mix well until all the ingredients are incorporated. Add the flour all at once and, with a fork or a pastry cutter, gently but swiftly work the mixture into a soft dough. Be careful not to overwork the dough, as it could become tough when cooked.

Lightly dust a medium bowl with flour. Add the dough and cover with plastic wrap. Refrigerate for at least 30 minutes.

Lightly flour a clean work surface and a large plate. Divide the dough into 3 or 4 parts, then roll each piece between your palms into a log ¾ inch/2 cm in diameter. Using a small knife or a pastry scraper, cut each log into ten to twelve 1-inch/2.5-cm pieces, then transfer these gnocchi to the plate and refrigerate them for 30 minutes, until chilled.

Bring a large pot of salted water to a boil on high heat. Add the gnocchi and cook them until they float, about 1 to 2 minutes. Drain and rinse the gnocchi. Transfer the gnocchi to a sauté pan, add the vegetable nage and heat on medium heat until the nage has nearly reduced by half, about 5 minutes. Turn off the heat and stir in the butter, chives and hazelnuts. Add half the pecorino Romano and toss gently.

TO SERVE Divide the gnocchi and sauce among 4 bowls.
Garnish with sage leaves and the remaining pecorino
Romano.

WINE Serve the best: Russian River Chardonnay or white
Burgundy, like Chassagne or Puligny-Montrachet; or,
if you must have red, mature Barbaresco or Brunello could
be magic.

Roasted Chicken *with* Braised Fennel *and* Watercress Salad

Serves 4

ROASTED CHICKEN

2 Tbsp	grapeseed oil	30 mL
2	whole chicken legs, each 7 to 9 oz/ 200 to 255 g	2
2	whole chicken breasts, each 9 to 10 oz/255 to 285 g, wing tips removed	2
1	carrot, cut in ¼-inch/5-mm dice	1
1 stalk	celery, cut in ¼-inch/5-mm dice	1 stalk
2	shallots, quartered	2
2 sprigs	fresh oregano	2 sprigs
1 cup	chicken stock (page 235)	250 mL
1 Tbsp	butter, chilled	15 mL

In this dish, the real star is the watercress; the chicken is the garnish. Braising the fennel allows all the flavours to stay in the pan and coat the softened pieces. Try this braising method with other vegetables, too.

ROASTED CHICKEN Preheat the oven to 375°F/190°C. Heat the grapeseed oil in a cast-iron pan or an ovenproof sauté pan on medium-high heat. Season the chicken legs and breasts with salt and pepper. Add them to the pan, skin side down, and sear until golden brown, about 4 minutes. Add the carrots, celery, shallots and oregano, shaking the pan so the vegetables settle into it. Leaving the chicken skin side down, place the pan in the oven and cook for 10 minutes.

Shake the pan, pour in the chicken stock, turn the chicken over and cook for 5 to 6 more minutes. To check for doneness, insert a knife or skewer into the thickest part of the leg, remove it, then push on the leg to release the juices. They should run clear. (A meat thermometer inserted into the thickest part of the leg should read 180°F/85°C.) Remove the pan from the oven, transfer the chicken legs and breasts to a plate and allow them to rest in a warm place for 5 to 10 minutes.

While the pan juices are still warm, strain them through a fine-mesh sieve into a medium bowl and discard the solids. Using a spoon, skim the fat off the surface. Add the butter to the juices, whisk well and set aside.

BRAISED FENNEL Cut each fennel half into thirds to obtain 12 pieces. Heat the olive oil in a deep sauté pan on medium heat. Add the fennel and sauté until lightly brown on both sides, about 6 minutes. Remove the pan from the heat.

Add the Pernod to the pan using a measuring spoon. (Pouring directly from the bottle into a hot pan can cause the vapours to lead back into the bottle and build enough pressure for the bottle to explode.) Return the pan to the heat, stand away from the stove and use a barbecue lighter or a long fireplace match to light the fumes at the edge of the pan. (Be careful to keep your hair and any loose clothing away from the pan, as the flames will rush up.) Allow the flames to burn for 2 minutes. If necessary, cover with a lid to put out the flames.

Add the fennel seeds and the bay leaf. Sauté for 2 minutes, then pour in the vegetable stock. Add the orange juice and zest and cook for 15 to 20 minutes until the stock is reduced to almost a syrup. Remove from the heat and keep warm.

WATERCRESS SALAD Place all the ingredients in a medium bowl and toss to combine. Season lightly with salt and pepper.

TO SERVE Divide the fennel among 4 bowls. With a sharp knife, cut the chicken drumsticks and thighs from the legs and slice the breasts in half. Arrange a piece of chicken leg and half a chicken breast over the fennel and spoon the pan juices over them. Finish each serving with a quarter of the watercress salad and drizzle with the dressing from the bowl.

WINE Choose Carneros Chardonnay or B.C. or Alsace Pinot Gris.

BRAISED FENNEL

2	medium fennel bulbs, halved and cores removed	2
2 Tbsp	olive oil	30 mL
1 Tbsp	Pernod or other anise-flavoured liqueur	15 mL
1 tsp	fennel seeds	5 mL
1	bay leaf	1
2 cups	vegetable stock (page 233)	500 mL
	Juice and zest of 1 orange	

WATERCRESS SALAD

2 ½ cups	watercress, large stems removed	600 mL
1	green apple, halved, cored and thinly sliced	1
2 Tbsp	slivered almonds, toasted	30 mL
1 Tbsp	apple cider vinegar	15 mL
2 Tbsp	olive oil	30 mL

Best Prime Rib Burgers *with* Spiced Ketchup *and* Taleggio Cheese

Serves 8 (Yields 8 5-oz/140-g patties)

SPICED KETCHUP

2 Tbsp	olive oil	30 mL
1	small onion, minced	1
1	jalapeño pepper, seeded and chopped	1
2 cloves	garlic, minced	2 cloves
2	red bell peppers, roasted, peeled, seeded and chopped	2
2 cups	canned plum tomatoes, crushed	500 mL
2 cups	tomato ketchup	500 mL
3 Tbsp	balsamic vinegar	45 mL
1 Tbsp	chopped fresh parsley	15 mL
1 Tbsp	chopped fresh basil	15 mL
1 tsp	ground cumin	5 mL
1½ tsp	cayenne pepper	7.5 mL
1 Tbsp	paprika	15 mL

Nothing says summer more than a barbecue, and during the warmer months we open our patio for a lunch service. Although we have tried different burger recipes over time, this one continues to be one of our favourites. The prime rib—often sold as rib roast—makes a very moist burger, and the semi-soft Taleggio cheese from Italy is wonderfully creamy.

SPICED KETCHUP Heat the olive oil in a medium saucepan on low heat. Add the onions and jalapeño peppers and sauté until soft and lightly coloured, about 5 minutes. Stir in the garlic and bell peppers and cook for 2 minutes, then add the tomatoes, ketchup, balsamic vinegar, parsley, basil, cumin, cayenne and paprika. Simmer for 15 to 20 minutes, then transfer the sauce to a clean bowl and refrigerate for 30 minutes until well chilled. Will keep refrigerated in an airtight container for up to 4 days.

PRIME RIB BURGERS In a large bowl, combine the prime rib, chuck, shallots, Dijon mustard, Worcestershire sauce and salt and mix well. Cover and refrigerate for 30 minutes, until well chilled.

Heat a barbecue or broiler to medium-high heat. Divide the beef mixture into 8 equal parts. Roll each portion into a ball, then shape into ¾-inch/2-cm thick patties. Oil the grill, then place the patties on it and cook for 6 to 8 minutes per side, or until medium-rare to medium. Toast the buns (or brioche slices).

TO SERVE In a small bowl, toss the arugula with the olive oil. Place half a bun on each plate, top with a burger and place a slice of cheese on top to soften while the patty is still warm. Garnish with slices of tomato, arugula and liberal amounts of spiced ketchup. Top with the remaining half of each bun. Serve immediately.

WINE A cold B.C. microbrewery beer would be ideal, but Sicilian Nero d'Avola or California Zinfandel wines would be great, too.

PRIME RIB BURGERS

1½ lbs	ground prime rib (rib roast)	680 g
1 lb	ground chuck	455 g
2	shallots, minced	2
2 Tbsp	Dijon mustard	30 mL
1 tsp	Worcestershire sauce	5 mL
1 Tbsp	kosher salt	15 mL
8	kaiser buns, halved, or 16 slices of brioche (page 242)	8
1½ cups	arugula, washed and dried	355 mL
1 Tbsp	olive oil	15 mL
8 slices	Taleggio cheese, each 1 oz/30 g	8 slices
2	beefsteak tomatoes, sliced	2

Seared Beef *with* Ratatouille *and* Onion Rings

Serves 4

DIABLE SAUCE

6	shallots, sliced	6
1 sprig	fresh thyme	1 sprig
1 sprig	fresh tarragon	1 sprig
1	bay leaf	1
1 Tbsp	black peppercorns	15 mL
¾ cup	white wine vinegar	185 mL
⅓ cup	white wine	80 mL
2 Tbsp	tomato paste	30 mL
½ tsp	cayenne pepper (optional)	2.5 mL
1½ cups	chicken stock (page 235)	375 mL
4 cups	veal demi-glace (page 234)	1 L
1 Tbsp	maple syrup	15 mL

ONION RINGS

2	large sweet onions, such as Walla Walla or Vidalia	2
2 cups	buttermilk	500 mL
½ cup	whipping cream	125 mL
2	eggs	2
1½ cups	dry bread crumbs	355 mL
½ tsp	cayenne pepper	2.5 mL
1 tsp	kosher salt	5 mL
½ cup	all-purpose flour	120 mL
12 cups	vegetable oil, for deep-frying	3 L

When I first met Bob Mitchell of Pemberton Meadows Natural Beef, I was reminded of what I like about farm folk. He, like all the farmers we deal with, is one of the friendliest, most genuine and down-to-earth people I know. And it's true: if you know the source of your food, it does taste twice as good.

The cayenne pepper in the diable sauce is optional but results in a spicier sauce. We use this sauce with roasted and pan-seared meats.

DIABLE SAUCE Combine the shallots, thyme, tarragon, bay leaf, peppercorns, white wine vinegar and white wine in a large saucepan on high heat. Reduce this mixture to a third, about 6 minutes. Add the tomato paste and cayenne and cook for 3 minutes. Reduce the heat to medium, pour in the chicken stock and veal demi-glace and bring to a boil. Reduce the heat to low and simmer until the sauce coats the back of a spoon, about 15 minutes. Strain the sauce through a fine-mesh sieve into a clean bowl, discarding any solids. Stir in the maple syrup and season lightly with salt. Will keep refrigerated in an airtight container for up to 1 week.

ONION RINGS On a clean work surface, peel the onions, discarding the skins, and slice into ½-inch/1-cm rings. Carefully separate the rings so as not to break too many of them. Transfer the onion rings to a shallow dish, cover them with the buttermilk and allow to stand for 45 minutes.

Drain the buttermilk into a small bowl, add the cream and eggs and mix well. In another small bowl, combine the bread crumbs, cayenne and salt. Place the flour in a third small bowl.

Dip the onions in the flour, then in the buttermilk mixture and finally in the bread crumb mixture. Arrange them on a baking sheet and refrigerate for 15 minutes, until chilled. Remove the chilled onion rings from the refrigerator, and repeat this battering and chilling once more, stacking the rings as necessary. Refrigerate until needed.

RATATOUILLE Heat olive oil in a large sauté pan on medium heat. Add the onions and sauté until soft and translucent, about 5 minutes. Add the eggplant and garlic and season lightly with salt and pepper. Increase the heat to high to evaporate the excess liquid, about 3 minutes. Once the eggplant is soft, reduce the heat to medium, add the zucchini and bell peppers and cook for 5 to 6 minutes, until the peppers are softened. Stir in the tomato paste and cook for 2 more minutes. Remove from the heat and add the diced tomatoes, basil and oregano (or marjoram) and season lightly with salt and pepper. Allow the ratatouille to cool. Will keep refrigerated in an airtight container for up to 3 days.

SEARED BEEF Preheat the oven to 400°F/205°C. Combine the salt and pepper in a small bowl and then sprinkle it onto a plate. Roll the tenderloin in the spice mixture until it is well coated on all sides.

continued overleaf...

RATATOUILLE

¼ cup	olive oil	60 mL
1	onion, diced	1
1	large eggplant, peeled and cut in small dice	1
2 cloves	garlic, minced	2 cloves
2	small zucchini, diced	2
2	red bell peppers, seeded and diced	2
1 Tbsp	tomato paste	15 mL
1 cup	diced tomatoes	250 mL
1 Tbsp	chopped fresh basil	15 mL
1 Tbsp	chopped fresh oregano or marjoram	15 mL

SEARED BEEF

1½ tsp	kosher salt	7.5 mL
1½ tsp	freshly cracked black pepper	7.5 mL
2 lbs	Pemberton beef tenderloin, trimmed of silver skin and tied into a small roast	900 g
2 Tbsp	grapeseed oil	30 mL
2 sprigs	fresh sage	2 sprigs
4	shallots, halved	4
2 cups	diable sauce	500 mL

In an ovenproof sauté pan, heat grapeseed oil on medium-high heat. Add the beef and sear for 2 to 3 minutes on each side to colour it. Remove the pan from the heat, add the sage and the shallots, then place the pan in the oven. Cook for 8 minutes, then turn the roast and cook for another 10 minutes, or until a thin knife or skewer inserted into the thickest part of the beef feels slightly warm to the touch. This indicates that the meat is medium-rare to medium.

Transfer the beef to a cool plate. Allow it to rest for 10 to 15 minutes, then remove the strings. Drain the oil, sage and shallots from the pan, then add the diable sauce and set aside.

FINISH ONION RINGS Fill a deep pot or a wok two-thirds full with vegetable oil and heat it to 330°F/165°C (use a deep-fat thermometer to check the temperature). Deep-fry the onion rings until golden brown and crisp, about 2 minutes per batch. Using a slotted spoon, remove the onion rings from the oil, drain on paper towels and season with salt and pepper.

TO SERVE Divide the ratatouille among 4 plates. Carve the beef into 8 or 12 slices and arrange 2 to 3 slices on top of the ratatouille on each plate. Spoon a quarter of the diable sauce over each serving of beef and around the plate. Garnish with the onion rings.

WINE Try a hearty Napa Cabernet Sauvignon, a savoury Super Tuscan (Merlot- or Cabernet-based), a yummy ripe Châteauneuf du Pape or a bold red from Priorat, Spain.

Loin *of* Lamb *with* Summer Squash *and* Sweet Peppers

Serves 4

GRILLED LAMB

2 Tbsp	extra-virgin olive oil	30 mL
	Juice of 1 lemon	
2 sprigs	fresh rosemary	2 sprigs
4	boneless lamb loins, each 8 to 9 oz/225 to 255 g, trimmed of fat and silver skin	4

The great thing about zucchini is that individual plants produce so many vegetables. These summer squash are best harvested when they are little and their skins are thin. In this dish, grilling them imparts a smoky taste that holds up to the flavour of lamb. Vincotto and saba are cooked grape must products that provide a tangy, vinegary flavour. If you cannot find either of them at your local fine grocery store, substitute aged balsamic vinegar.

GRILLED LAMB Preheat the barbecue or grill to medium. In a small bowl, mix the olive oil and lemon juice. Strip the rosemary leaves from the stems and discard the stems. Roughly chop the leaves and add them to the oil mixture. Rub the oil mixture over the lamb and season with the salt and pepper.

Grill the lamb loins for 3 minutes, then turn them 90° to create a pattern of crossed grill marks on the meat and cook for another 2 minutes. Turn the loins over and repeat on the other side. Remove the lamb from the grill and allow it to rest for 5 to 10 minutes. The lamb should be cooked medium-rare to medium. To be sure, cut into the centre of one piece to check that it is pink but not bloody. Set lamb aside.

continued overleaf...

GRILLED SQUASH AND PEPPERS Preheat a barbecue or grill to high. Combine the zucchini and bell peppers in a bowl, then add 3 Tbsp/45 mL of the olive oil and the thyme. Season lightly with salt and pepper and toss until the vegetables are well coated. Place the bell peppers on the grill and cook for 2 to 3 minutes per side. Add the zucchini, grilling them for 1 to 2 minutes per side. The vegetables should be well marked and slightly charred. Return the cooked vegetables to the bowl, add the vincotto (or saba), cover and set aside.

Heat the remaining olive oil in a sauté pan on medium heat, add the polenta and cook until each piece is golden brown on all sides, 3 to 4 minutes. Remove the polenta from the heat and set aside. In a small saucepan, heat the red wine sauce until it is warmed through.

TO SERVE Arrange a quarter of the mixed squash and peppers in the centre of each plate. Top with a slice of polenta. Thinly slice the lamb loins across the grain and fan the slices over the polenta. Drizzle with the red wine sauce and the basil oil, then finish by spooning with a quarter of the caponata over each serving.

WINE Coonawarra Cabernet Sauvignon, top-quality Bordeaux or even Australian Shiraz will stand up to the tangy caponata and the flavourful meat.

GRILLED SQUASH AND PEPPERS

10 to 12	baby zucchini (assorted colours), halved lengthwise	10 to 12
7 to 8	small sweet bell peppers (assorted colours), halved and seeded	7 to 8
¼ cup	extra-virgin olive oil	60 mL
1 tsp	thyme leaves	5 mL
1 Tbsp	vincotto or saba	15 mL
4 pieces	Parmesan polenta, each 1 × 3½ inches/ 2.5 × 9 cm (page 205)	4 pieces
1 cup	red wine sauce (page 239)	250 mL
2 Tbsp	basil oil (page 235)	30 mL
½ cup	caponata (page 67)	120 mL

Casserole of Baby Vegetables *with* Pork Belly *and* Tomato Marmalade

Serves 6

PORK BELLY

2 Tbsp	coriander seeds	30 mL
1 Tbsp	fennel seeds	15 mL
3	whole star anise	3
1 Tbsp	pickling spice	15 mL
1 Tbsp	black peppercorns	15 mL
6 Tbsp	kosher salt	90 mL
4 lbs	pork belly, skin on	1.8 kg
2 Tbsp	grapeseed oil	30 mL
1	large carrot, cut in ½-inch/1-cm dice	1
1	medium onion, cut in ½-inch/1-cm dice	1
2 stalks	celery, cut in ½-inch/1-cm dice	2 stalks
8 cups	vegetable or chicken stock (pages 233, 235)	2 L
1 cup	tomato marmalade (page 238)	250 mL
6 sprigs	fresh oregano, for garnish	6 sprigs

At first glance, this recipe seems hard, but it is really very easy—it's just a matter of patience. The pork is so tender and moist that it is well worth the wait. Cook the pork with whatever vegetables you have on hand and use the ones you really love for the casserole.

PORK BELLY In a small saucepan, combine the coriander seeds, fennel seeds, star anise, pickling spice and peppercorns and toast lightly on low heat until their scent becomes very strong and they begin to colour, about 4 minutes. Remove from the heat. Allow the spices to cool slightly, then transfer them to a spice grinder (or a coffee grinder) and grind them to a sandy texture. In a small bowl, combine the ground spices and the salt and mix well.

Sprinkle one-third of the spice mixture in a shallow pan large enough to hold the pork belly. Using a sharp knife, score the skin of the pork belly ¼-inch/5-mm deep in a cross-hatch pattern. Place the pork in the baking pan, then rub the remaining spice mixture into the pork. Cover the pan with plastic wrap, then set a large pan on top of the pork, wrap and weight it with 2 or 3 large cans of vegetables. Refrigerate the pork belly for 48 hours.

continued overleaf...

Preheat the oven to 300°F/150°C. Once the pork belly has cured, remove the weights, the pan and the wrap. With a paper towel, wipe off the excess spice mixture. In a large pot or a deep ovenproof baking dish large enough to hold the pork, heat the grapeseed oil on medium heat. Add the carrots, onions and celery and sauté to release the flavours, 7 to 8 minutes. Add the pork belly and the vegetable (or chicken) stock, then pour in enough water to just cover the pork. Increase the heat to high, until the stock comes to a boil. Cover the pot (or the baking dish) with a lid (or with parchment paper and then aluminum foil), transfer to the oven and cook for 3¼ hours. When the pork is done, it will be very tender.

Using two slotted spoons, transfer the pork from the braising liquid to a clean work surface. Discard the braising liquid; it is too salty to use for any other purpose. Allow the pork to cool until it can be handled, then use a spatula or a spoon to scrape off the scored skin and most of the excess fat. Discard this skin and fat.

Cut a piece of plastic wrap that is 6 inches/15 cm longer than the pork belly. Slightly moisten a clean work surface with water and place the plastic wrap on top, with a long edge toward you. Arrange the pork in the centre of the plastic wrap so that the long grains of the meat lie perpendicular to you (this will allow you to slice the pork against the grain). Fold the edge of the plastic wrap nearest you over the pork, then tightly roll the pork in the plastic wrap to create a log shape. Grasp the plastic wrap at both ends of the log and twist them to make the log as tight as possible. Refrigerate the pork for at least 8 hours.

VEGETABLE CASSEROLE In a large sauté pan, heat the butter on medium heat until it melts. Add the pearl onions and bacon and sauté for 2 minutes to release the oils. Add the chanterelles, toss to coat them with the butter and cook for 4 to 5 minutes. Stir in the carrots and turnips and season very lightly with salt. Pour in the vegetable nage and cook on medium heat until the liquid is reduced by half, about 5 minutes. Add the cauliflower and continue cooking until the liquid is reduced to barely a quarter of its original volume, then add the rosemary and honey. The vegetables should be quite tender and the jus sweet and flavourful. Remove from the heat, cover and set aside.

FINISH PORK BELLY Slice the pork belly into six even slices. Heat a sauté pan on medium-low heat, then add the pork. No oil is needed, as the pork will release some fats and naturally colour. Cook for 5 to 6 minutes per side, until the meat is soft to the touch and nicely browned.

TO SERVE Divide the vegetables among six individual bowls and top with a slice of pork. Garnish each serving of pork with a quenelle of tomato marmalade and a sprig of oregano.

WINE Among the many possibilities are Oregon Pinot Noir, red Burgundy (like Chambolle-Musigny), a high-acid Italian red like modern Barolo or Chianti Classico, or fuller whites such as Austrian Grüner Veltliner. Grand cru Alsatian Riesling or Pinot Gris are also natural choices with rich pork dishes.

VEGETABLE CASSEROLE

2 Tbsp	unsalted butter	30 mL
10 to 12	pearl onions, peeled	10 to 12
1 oz	bacon, blanched and minced (about 2 to 3 slices)	30 g
1 cup	chanterelle mushrooms, brushed and scraped of any dirt	240 mL
8 to 10	globe carrots or baby carrots, peeled and halved	8 to 10
8 to 10	baby turnips, peeled and quartered	8 to 10
2 cups	vegetable nage (page 233)	500 mL
1 cup	cauliflower florets	240 mL
1 tsp	rosemary leaves	5 mL
2 Tbsp	fireweed honey	30 mL

Peach *and* Brandy Soup *with* Sour Cream Ice Cream

Serves 8 (4-oz/115-g servings) as a dessert

PEACH PURÉE

5 lbs	whole ripe peaches	2.25 kg
1	vanilla bean, pod split and seeds scraped	1
	Juice of 1 lemon	

PEACH AND BRANDY SOUP

½ cup	brandy	125 mL
1	vanilla bean, pod split and seeds scraped	1
¼ cup	superfine (caster) sugar	60 mL
6	black peppercorns, crushed	6
2 cups	peach purée, chilled	500 mL
½ cup	Champagne or sweet sparkling wine	125 mL
	Juice of 1½ lemons	
2	ripe peaches, blanched and skin removed, for garnish	2
8 sprigs	fresh mint or anise hyssop, for garnish	8 sprigs

SOUR CREAM ICE CREAM

4 cups	sour cream (do not use low-fat or no-fat varieties)	1 L
1¼ cups	granulated sugar	300 mL
	Juice of 2 lemons	
⅓ cup	whipping cream	80 mL

The peaches and other stone fruit grown in the Okanagan are exceptional, and this dish really highlights the peach's flavour. Dessert soups add a nice light touch to the end of any meal and can be dressed up with a caramelized puff pastry lattice, as we do at the restaurant. I learned this ice cream recipe, which uses no eggs, while at chef school and I use it all the time.

PEACH PURÉE With a clean, dry towel, rub the fuzz off the peaches. Cut the peaches in half and discard the pits. Leave the skins on. Place the fruit and the vanilla in a large saucepan and cook on medium-low heat, stirring frequently, until the peaches are just soft, about 10 minutes. Stir in the lemon juice. Discard the vanilla pod.

Transfer the mixture to a food processor and purée until smooth, or blend with a hand-held blender. Pass the peach purée through a fine-mesh sieve into a clean bowl and refrigerate until chilled, about 1 hour. Will keep refrigerated in an airtight container for up to 3 days.

PEACH AND BRANDY SOUP Combine brandy, vanilla, sugar and peppercorns in a small saucepan on low heat. Bring to a boil and simmer gently for 2 to 3 minutes, then remove from the heat and allow to cool. Strain the mixture through a fine-mesh sieve into a clean bowl and discard the solids.

Pour the peach purée into a bowl. Stir in the brandy mixture, Champagne (or sparkling wine) and two-thirds of the lemon juice until well mixed. Refrigerate for 1 hour.

SOUR CREAM ICE CREAM Combine all of the ingredients in a large bowl and whisk until smooth. Allow the mixture to stand for 30 minutes to dissolve the sugar. Transfer the mixture to an ice cream maker and process according to the manufacturer's directions.

TO SERVE Chill 8 small bowls. Halve the blanched peaches
and discard the pits. Cut the peaches into 1-inch/1-cm dice.
In a small bowl, toss the peach cubes with the remaining lemon juice to prevent oxidization. Divide the diced
peaches among the bowls. Ladle the brandy and peach
soup on top and garnish with a scoop of sour cream
ice cream and a sprig of mint (or anise hyssop). Serve
immediately.

WINE Moscato d'Asti would be perfect, and not too sweet.

Summer Berry Pavlova *with* Lavender Cream

Serves 8

LAVENDER CREAM

1 cup	whipping cream	250 mL
2 Tbsp	dried lavender	30 mL
1	vanilla bean, seeds scraped and pod discarded	1
1 tsp	granulated sugar	5 mL

MERINGUES

13	large egg whites, at room temperature	13
¼ tsp	salt	1 mL
2 ½ cups	superfine (caster) sugar	600 mL
1 ½ Tbsp	cornstarch	25 mL
1 ½ Tbsp	white vinegar	25 mL

We prepared this dish for a Feast of Fields event at North Arm Farm in Pemberton several years ago and have since featured it on our menu at various times. This recipe is great for its simplicity and for showing off the flavour of the ripe berries.

LAVENDER CREAM In a small bowl, combine the cream and the lavender. Cover and refrigerate the lavender cream for at least 12 hours to allow the flavours to infuse. Will keep refrigerated in an airtight container for up to 2 days.

MERINGUES Preheat the oven to 250°F/120°C. Line a baking sheet with parchment paper.

Place the egg whites and salt in the bowl of an electric mixer fitted with a whisk attachment. Beat the whites at high speed until they form soft peaks, about 5 minutes. With the mixer on low speed, gradually add 2 cups/480 mL of the sugar, then increase the speed to medium-high and whip until the meringue forms stiff, glossy peaks, about 5 minutes.

In a small bowl, combine the remaining ½ cup/120 mL sugar and the cornstarch. With the electric mixer on low speed, add this mixture to the meringue and process until well incorporated. Mix in the white vinegar.

Using a large serving spoon, drop the meringue onto the baking sheet, forming 8 mounds, each roughly 2 inches/5 cm high (each pavlova will use about ½ cup/ 120 mL of the meringue). Press down on the top of each meringue with the back of the spoon to make a concave depression. Bake for 1 to 1¼ hours, or until the meringues are crisp on the outside and soft on the inside. Allow the meringues to cool on a wire rack for 30 minutes before serving.

FRUIT TOPPING Combine the raspberries, strawberries, blueberries and red currants in a large bowl with 2 Tbsp/30 mL of the raspberry coulis. Set aside.

FINISH LAVENDER CREAM Strain the lavender cream through a fine-mesh sieve and discard the lavender. Place the lavender cream, vanilla and sugar in the bowl of an electric mixer fitted with a whisk attachment. Beat at high speed until the cream forms firm peaks, about 5 minutes.

TO SERVE Pour a small drop of raspberry coulis into the centre of each plate. Arrange a meringue on top of the coulis. Fill the hollow of each meringue with an eighth of the lavender cream and arrange the mixed berries around the cream. Generously drizzle raspberry coulis around each plate, on either side of the meringue. Lightly dust the pavlovas with icing sugar.

WINE The rare but delicious and lightly sweet red fizz from Piedmonte—Brachetto d'Acqui—would be magic, or try California Black Muscat.

FRUIT TOPPING

1 cup	fresh raspberries	240 mL
1 cup	fresh strawberries, halved	240 mL
1 cup	fresh blueberries	240 mL
½ cup	fresh red currants, stemmed	120 mL
1 cup	raspberry coulis (page 98)	250 mL
2 Tbsp	icing sugar	30 mL

Nougat Glacé *with* Blueberries *and* Pistachio Praline

Serves 8

The creaminess of the frozen nougat pairs particularly well with the earthy sweetness of the blueberries in this late-summer dessert. It is further enhanced by the pistachio praline, which our pastry chef, Aaron Heath, adds for a nice textural contrast. You can also make this dessert with almonds instead of pistachios—both work well. For a more elegant presentation, garnish the nougat glacé with a crisp tuile or a pre-made cigar-shaped pastry.

PISTACHIO PRALINE Preheat the oven to 340°F/170°C. Line a baking sheet with parchment paper. Arrange the pistachios on the baking sheet and toast until very light brown, about 10 minutes. Remove from the oven and allow the nuts to cool on the baking sheet.

In a small pot, combine the sugar with just enough water to moisten it evenly (about ¼ cup/60 mL). Heat the sugar on medium heat, without stirring, until it is caramelized and a light amber in colour, about 10 minutes. Pour this syrup over the pistachios and stir gently until the nuts are evenly coated. Allow the praline to cool completely, then grind it in batches in a food processor until you have a fine powder.

NOUGAT GLACÉ Lightly grease eight 1½-inch/4-cm ring moulds and line them with parchment paper. Arrange the prepared ring moulds on a small baking sheet.

Pour the egg whites into the bowl of an electric mixer fitted with a whisk attachment. In a small pot, combine the sugar with just enough water to moisten it evenly (about ¼ cup/60 mL). Bring the sugar to a gentle boil on medium heat, then continue cooking it, without stirring, for about 10 minutes, until the sugar mixture reaches 243°F/117°C (use a candy thermometer to check the temperature).

continued overleaf...

PISTACHIO PRALINE

⅛ cup	shelled pistachios	30 mL
⅛ cup	granulated sugar	30 mL

NOUGAT GLACÉ

2 ½	egg whites, at room temperature	2 ½
½ cup	granulated sugar	120 mL
½ cup	whipping cream	125 mL
1 recipe	pistachio praline	1 recipe
2 cups	fresh blueberries	480 mL
1 Tbsp	amaretto or other almond liqueur	15 mL
¼ cup	slivered pistachios, toasted, for garnish	60 mL
8 sprigs	fresh mint, for garnish	8 sprigs

1 ⅛ lbs	whole apricots, skin on	500 g
½ cup + 1 tsp	granulated sugar	125 mL
½	vanilla bean, pod split and seeds scraped	½
	Juice of 1 lemon	

While the sugar is cooking, start beating the egg whites on medium speed. Beat them until they form soft peaks, about 5 minutes. With the electric mixer still set on medium speed, slowly pour the warm syrup down the inside edge of the mixer bowl. Increase the speed to high and whip the egg whites until the bottom of the bowl is cool to the touch, about 5 minutes. Set aside.

In a separate bowl, whip the cream until it forms soft peaks, about 5 minutes. Fold one-third of the whipped cream into the meringue mixture to lighten it, then fold in the remaining whipped cream and the pistachio praline until well combined. Spoon this mixture into a piping bag fitted with a wide nozzle. Pipe one-eighth of the cream mixture into each ring mould, then freeze the moulds for 2 hours. Will keep tightly wrapped in plastic wrap and frozen for up to 3 days.

APRICOT COULIS Halve the apricots and discard the pits. Do not peel. Place the apricots, sugar and vanilla bean in a small pot and cook on medium-low heat, stirring frequently, until the apricots are just soft, about 6 minutes. Stir in the lemon juice. Discard the vanilla pod.

Transfer the mixture to a food processor and purée until smooth, or blend with a hand-held blender. Pass the coulis through a fine-mesh sieve into a clean bowl and refrigerate until chilled, about 1 hour. Will keep refrigerated in an airtight container for up to 3 days.

TO SERVE Place the blueberries in a small bowl, add the amaretto (or other liqueur) and toss gently until well combined. Dab a spoonful of the apricot coulis onto the centre of each plate. Gently unmould the nougats and place one on each serving of coulis. Arrange the blueberries on top of and around each nougat. Drizzle the dishes with 2 more spoonfuls of the apricot coulis and garnish with slivered pistachios and a sprig of mint.

WINE Any kind of sweet Muscat would be nice here, like Muscat de Beaumes-de-Venise, Muscat de Rivesaltes or an Australian liqueur Muscat.

Raspberry Sablés *with* Raspberry Coulis *and* Chantilly Cream

Serves 6

PÂTE SABLÉ

13 ½ oz	all-purpose flour, sifted (about 3 ¾ cups/900 mL)	380 g
7 oz	icing sugar (about ⅞ cup/210 mL)	200 g
1 tsp	salt	5 mL
1	vanilla bean, seeds scraped and pod discarded	1
14 oz	unsalted butter (about 1 ⅔ cups/ 400 mL), softened and cut in 1-inch/ 2.5-cm cubes	400 g
1 tsp	whipping cream	5 mL
1	egg yolk	1

RASPBERRY COULIS

2 cups	fresh raspberries	480 mL
½ cup	granulated sugar	120 mL
	Juice of 1 lemon	

We are fortunate enough to have acclaimed pastry chef Thierry Busset working in our Top Table restaurant group. This simple dessert is based on a dish he has been making for many years and really captures the true flavour of raspberries. At Araxi, we garnish the sablés with a small cone of raspberry fruit leather and a seasonal herb garnish. Enjoy.

PÂTE SABLÉ Combine the flour, icing sugar, salt and vanilla in a bowl using a whisk. Add the butter and incorporate, using your fingers or a pastry cutter, until the mixture resembles coarse oatmeal or wet sand. Make a well in the centre of the bowl, then pour in the cream and the egg yolk. Combine gently until the dough just comes together, then transfer it to a clean work surface and flatten it into a round 1-inch/2.5-cm thick. Tightly wrap the dough in plastic wrap and refrigerate it for 1 hour until chilled.

Line a baking sheet with parchment paper and lightly flour a clean work surface. Unwrap the sablé dough, place it on the floured surface and roll it to a thickness of ⅛ inch/ 3 mm. Using a 3-inch/7.5-cm round cutter, cut out 12 discs. Place the rounds on the baking sheet and refrigerate them for 30 minutes.

Heat the oven to 350°F/175°C. Bake the sablés for 5 minutes or until golden brown, then transfer them to a wire rack and allow them to cool.

RASPBERRY COULIS Place the raspberries, sugar and lemon juice in a medium saucepan and cook on medium heat, stirring constantly, until the mixture comes to a gentle boil. Simmer for 5 minutes, or until the coulis begins to thicken slightly.

continued overleaf...

CHANTILLY CREAM

1 cup	whipping cream	250 mL
1 tsp	granulated sugar	5 mL
1	vanilla bean, seeds scraped and pod discarded	1
4 cups	fresh raspberries	1 L
¼ cup	icing sugar, for dusting	60 mL

While it is still warm, transfer the mixture to a food processor and purée until smooth, or blend with a hand-held blender. Pass the coulis through a fine-mesh sieve into a clean bowl and refrigerate until chilled, about 1 hour. Will keep refrigerated in an airtight container for up to 3 days.

CHANTILLY CREAM Combine the cream, sugar and vanilla in the bowl of an electric mixer fitted with a whisk attachment. Whip at high speed until the mixture forms stiff peaks, about 10 minutes.

TO SERVE Place the raspberries in a large bowl and toss with ¼ cup/60 mL of the raspberry coulis. Arrange a ring of berries, about the diameter of one of the sablé discs, in the middle of each plate. Fill the centre of the ring with two spoonfuls of chantilly cream. Top the cream with a sablé disc. Repeat with a second layering of berries, cream and a sablé disc. Lightly dust each serving with icing sugar.

WINE I pair raspberries with a dessert wine from Veneto, Italy: Maculan's Dindarello; if you can't find it, try a late-harvest B.C. Riesling.

Everbearing Strawberry Tart

Serves 6

North Arm Farm in Pemberton grows a type of strawberry called a day-neutral that bears fruit until the first frost, and our guests are often shocked to be eating local strawberries in September and October. Although the autumn crop is generally not as sweet as the early summer harvest in June and July, the later strawberries make a lovely tart, which we serve with a sweet pastry cream.

SWEET SHORTCRUST PASTRY Place the butter and sugar in the bowl of an electric mixer fitted with a paddle attachment and beat at medium-high speed until smooth and creamy, about 5 minutes. Add the vanilla. With the mixer on low speed, gradually add the beaten eggs, turning off the mixer two or three times to scrape down the sides of the bowl.

Lightly flour a clean work surface. Combine the flour and salt in a medium bowl. With the mixer at its lowest speed, add the flour mixture in 3 or 4 batches, being sure to completely incorporate one batch before adding another. Turn off the mixer when the pastry comes together in a crumbly mass.

Transfer the dough to the floured surface and knead it briefly until it becomes smooth. Flatten the dough into a round 1-inch/2.5-cm thick, tightly wrap it in plastic wrap and refrigerate for 1 hour, until chilled.

Preheat the oven to 350°F/175°C. Line a baking sheet with parchment paper and lightly flour a clean work surface. Unwrap the dough, place it on the floured surface and knead it briefly until the dough is soft and pliable but still cool. Keeping the surface lightly dusted with flour, roll the dough evenly to a thickness of ⅛ inch/3 mm. Using a

continued overleaf...

SWEET SHORTCRUST PASTRY

9 oz	unsalted butter, softened (about 1⅛ cups/270 mL)	255 g
6½ oz	superfine (caster) sugar (about ⅞ cup/210 mL)	185 g
1	vanilla bean, seeds scraped and pod discarded	1
2	large eggs, lightly beaten	2
1⅛ lbs	all-purpose flour, sifted (about 2¼ cups/540 mL)	500 g
1 tsp	salt	5 mL

VANILLA PASTRY CREAM

6	egg yolks	6
2 Tbsp	all-purpose flour, sifted	30 mL
1 Tbsp	cornstarch	15 mL
½ cup	granulated sugar	120 mL
2 cups	whole milk	500 mL
1	Tahitian vanilla bean, seeds scraped and pod discarded	1

5-inch/12.5-cm round cutter, cut out 6 discs. If the dough is too soft to handle, briefly return the discs to the refrigerator. Place the rounds into individual ring moulds, pressing the pastry into the corners and allowing any excess dough to hang over the edges of the moulds. Set the moulds on the baking sheet and refrigerate them for 10 minutes.

Blind-bake the dough by lining each mould with aluminum foil, filling it with baking beans or pie weights and baking the pastry shells for 10 to 12 minutes, until the edges are golden brown. Remove the baking beans (or pie weights) and the aluminum foil and return the moulds to the oven for another 2 to 3 minutes, until the bases of the shells are pale gold. Remove the moulds from the oven and allow the pastry to cool to room temperature. Remove the pastry shells from the moulds.

VANILLA PASTRY CREAM Fill a large bowl with ice. Place the egg yolks, flour, cornstarch and 2 oz/60 g of the sugar in a bowl and whisk until well combined. In a medium saucepan, combine the milk and vanilla, then add the remaining sugar. Bring the milk mixture to a boil on high heat. Carefully whisk ¼ cup/60 mL of the milk mixture into the yolk mixture to temper it. Gradually add the rest of the milk mixture, whisking constantly until smooth.

Pour the custard back into the saucepan. Reduce the heat to medium and bring the mixture to a boil, stirring constantly, then cook it for 2 minutes. The mixture will thicken considerably. Remove from the heat and strain the custard through a fine-mesh sieve into a medium bowl. Place the bowl of custard into the bowl of ice, cover with plastic wrap (press the wrap onto the surface of the mixture to prevent it from forming a skin on top) and allow the pastry cream to cool, stirring occasionally. Will keep refrigerated in an airtight container for up to 3 days.

STRAWBERRY COULIS Place the strawberries, sugar and lemon juice in a medium saucepan and cook on medium heat, stirring occasionally, until the berries are completely softened, about 4 minutes.

While it is still warm, transfer the mixture to a food processor and purée until smooth, or blend with a hand-held blender. Pass the coulis through a fine-mesh sieve into a clean bowl and refrigerate until chilled, about 1 hour. Will keep refrigerated in an airtight container for up to 3 days.

GRAND MARNIER CREAM Pour the pastry cream into a large bowl and whisk until smooth. Add the Grand Marnier and stir to combine.

Pour the whipping cream into the bowl of an electric mixer fitted with a whisk attachment and beat at high speed until the cream forms soft peaks, about 5 minutes. Using a spatula, fold one-third of the whipped cream into the pastry cream until combined. Gently fold in the remaining whipped cream. Refrigerate until needed.

STRAWBERRY TOPPING Place the strawberries in a medium bowl and toss with the Grand Marnier. Set aside.

TO SERVE Arrange a tart shell on each plate. Fill the crust with a sixth of the Grand Marnier cream. Garnish each tart with the strawberry topping and drizzle the plate with strawberry coulis before serving.

WINE With the Grand Marnier flavour accenting the strawberries, try California Orange Muscat or enjoy sipping some Grand Marnier from a snifter.

STRAWBERRY COULIS

1 ⅛ lbs	strawberries, cleaned and stemmed	500 g
½ cup + 1 tsp	granulated sugar	125 mL
	Juice of 1 lemon	

GRAND MARNIER CREAM

½ recipe	vanilla pastry cream, cold	½ recipe
2 Tbsp	Grand Marnier	30 mL
½ cup	whipping cream	125 mL

STRAWBERRY TOPPING

2 cups	strawberries, halved	480 mL
1 Tbsp	Grand Marnier	15 mL

Poached Apricots *with* Hazelnut Financiers

Serves 6

If you have never eaten a financier before, try to make this dessert—it is particularly easy and tasty. Traditionally, these cakes are made with almonds, but hazelnuts from Agassiz work very well in this recipe. Apricots are sometimes overlooked in favour of more popular fruits but they have a floral flavour not found in peaches or nectarines. This floral element pairs well with hazelnuts.

POACHED APRICOTS Combine the brandy, simple syrup, white wine, vanilla and orange zest in a medium saucepan and bring to a boil on high heat. Remove from the heat and keep warm.

Fill a large bowl with ice water. Fill a medium pot with water and bring it to a boil on high heat. Using a sharp knife, score the bottom of each apricot with a small X. Immerse the apricots in the boiling water for 15 seconds, or until the skin starts to loosen. Using a slotted spoon, plunge the apricots into the ice water to stop the cooking and allow them to cool. Remove the apricots from the water, pat them dry and discard the skins.

Cut the apricots in half, discard the pits and add the fruit to the reserved brandied poaching liquid. Return this mixture to low heat and simmer gently for 5 to 8 minutes, or until the apricots are soft. Remove from the heat. Using a slotted spoon, transfer the apricots to a clean bowl and refrigerate for 30 minutes until chilled. Strain the poaching liquid through a fine-mesh sieve and reserve it for the hazelnut financiers.

continued overleaf...

POACHED APRICOTS

⅞ cup	brandy	215 mL
1 cup	simple syrup (page 239)	250 mL
⅔ cup	white wine	165 mL
1	vanilla bean, pod split and seeds scraped	1
2 pieces	orange zest, each 2 inches/ 5 cm in length	2 pieces
12	whole ripe apricots, skin on	12

8 oz	unsalted butter (about 1 cup/240 mL) + 2 Tbsp/30 mL for coating moulds	225 g
2 Tbsp	granulated sugar	30 mL
3 oz	ground hazelnuts (about ⅜ cup/90 mL) + 1 Tbsp/15 mL for garnish	85 g
10 oz	icing sugar, sifted (about 1¼ cups/ 300 mL)	285 g
3 oz	all-purpose flour, sifted (about ⅜ cup/ 90 mL)	85 g
1	vanilla bean, seeds scraped and pod discarded	1
8 oz	egg whites (7 to 8), at room temperature	225 g
	reserved apricot poaching liquid	
1 cup	apricot coulis (page 96), for garnish	250 mL
6 sprigs	fresh mint, for garnish	6 sprigs

HAZELNUT FINANCIERS Lightly butter six 2-oz/60-mL savarin moulds with the 2 Tbsp/30 mL butter and sprinkle with the granulated sugar. Arrange the moulds on a small baking sheet.

Place a small stainless steel bowl in the freezer. Cut the remaining butter into 1-inch/2.5-cm cubes, place the cubes in a medium saucepan on high heat and melt them, whisking constantly. The butter will foam and then subside. Continue cooking the butter on high heat until it becomes golden brown and gives off a nutty aroma. This is a brown butter, or *beurre noisette*. Remove the brown butter from the heat and transfer it to the chilled bowl. Allow the butter to cool to room temperature, stirring frequently so the butter remains smooth.

In a large bowl, combine the ⅜ cup/90 mL of hazelnuts with the icing sugar, flour and vanilla. Using a rubber spatula, gradually stir in the egg whites until they are fully combined. Fold in the brown butter and mix well. Refrigerate the batter for 1 hour, until it is chilled.

Preheat the oven to 350°F/175°C. Transfer the batter to a piping bag fitted with a wide nozzle and pipe each savarin mould two-thirds full (or just spoon the batter into the individual moulds). Bake for 6 minutes, then turn the moulds around to ensure even cooking and bake for 3 to 5 minutes more, or until the cakes are golden brown. The cakes are cooked when a skewer or toothpick inserted into the thickest part comes out clean. Remove the financiers from the oven.

Line a baking sheet with parchment paper. Invert the cakes onto the baking sheet. While they are still warm, briefly dip each financier into the reserved apricot poaching liquid.

TO SERVE Spoon a sixth of the apricot coulis into the centre of each plate. Top with a dipped financier, then arrange 2 poached apricot halves on each cake. Sprinkle each serving with ground hazelnuts and garnish with a sprig of mint.

WINE This treat is perfect with B.C.'s fabulous ice wines, such as the consistently great ones by Quail's Gate, Nk'Mip Cellars and Inniskillin Winery.

HARVEST

··· *menu* ···

Butternut Squash Soup
with Pumpkin Seed Oil · 115

·······································

Roasted Beet Salad *with* Hazelnut
Dressing *and* Beet Chips · 116

·······································

Rock Sole *with* Pemberton Potato
Rösti *and* Lillooct Corn Sauce · 120

·······································

Roasted Pork Rack *with* Apple-Rosemary
Sauce *and* Sunchoke Purée · 123

·······································

Roasted Pear *with* Lillooet
Honey *and* Pear Sorbet · 126

Fields thick with ripening corn, potatoes waiting to be dug up and grapes heavy on the vine announce the beginning of autumn. The slight chill in the morning air means that the harvest is near. At Araxi, this is one of the busiest times of the year, as the restaurant showcases the region's bounty with special tasting menus based exclusively on items grown, produced and harvested within 100 miles. These menus epitomize Araxi's commitment to local, seasonal food and to the food- and wine-producing communities that support the restaurant all year round.

For gastronomes, the harvest is one of the most exciting times to visit Whistler and the Pemberton Valley. August brings the Slow Food Cycle Tour, an annual event that sees upwards of 2,000 people bicycling from one Pemberton farm to the next to sample the region's fresh produce. At Araxi, such vegetables as sunchokes, parsnips, beets, parsley roots and fifteen varieties of potatoes can be served fresh from the farms. At this time of year, a kaleidoscope of beets becomes a salad accented with toasted hazelnuts and their cold-pressed oils. Rock sole fillets are served on peaches-and-cream corn and topped with crisp potato rösti. Roasted pears from D'Arcy are caramelized with fireweed honey from Lillooet.

Now, the focus is on wine as much as on food—and it is Cornucopia, Whistler's premier culinary event, that takes centre stage. Since 1996 the annual celebration has grown each year and it consistently pushes the chefs and sommeliers to come up with spectacular menus. Restaurant director Steve Edwards explains: "For this event, which features the best vintages from such industry heavyweights as Kendall-Jackson and Penfolds

along with B.C. wineries, we reverse the usual process of matching wine to food. As a team, we help James create dishes that best suit each wine." Then, in true bacchanalian spirit, the restaurant stages a standing-room-only party with sparkling wines from B.C. and around the globe.

On the farms, in the village, at the restaurant, the harvest is a time of transition. The days, though shorter, still recall the warmth of summer. The kitchen staff uses a food dehydrator and a vacuum-pack machine to preserve summer fruit and berries at their peak. But the evenings bring cooler temperatures, light drizzle and the first dusting of snow on the mountains. The mist in the valley comes and goes, showing off the peaks then wrapping them up again. The farmers begin to cellar their root crops and bring their animals in from the pasture.

"Fall in Pemberton is one of my favourite times of the year," says executive chef James Walt. "Bob Mitchell's Pemberton Meadows beef is ready to be dry-aged for 48 days. And that's something to look forward to. That beef held its own against a Penfolds '98 Grange." He continues, "There is great local seafood, and the root crops in Pemberton are at their prime. The produce is right here in my backyard, and I can draw from fruit we put away in the summer, freshly dug crosnes and butter potatoes, and freshly harvested game meats like rabbit and venison.

The mushroom pickers are foraging. There's a lot to work with in the fall."

Pastry chef Aaron Heath features fall-fruit pastries, artisan cheeses and chocolates: "There's an old orchard that one of our suppliers came across a few years ago that has these fantastic apples and heirloom varieties of pears. They need very little to bring out the sweetness: a salty cheese, a few minutes of caramelization or a hint of chocolate."

The harvest season is busy at the farms, a time that pits farmers in a race against the first frost. At the restaurant, there are day-trippers stopping in for dinner after a walk in the woods and business people popping by the bar for a drink, but it's a time for reflection, for restocking, for anticipating the busy winter season. At Araxi, the room is warmly lit and the staff, as always, are ready to welcome you with the bounties of fall.

Butternut Squash Soup *with* Pumpkin Seed Oil

Serves 6 as an appetizer, 12 as an amuse-bouche (Yields 10 cups/2.5 L)

½ cup	unsalted butter	120 mL
2	shallots, sliced	2
5 lbs	butternut squash (about 2 small), peeled, seeded and thinly sliced	2.25 kg
7 cups	chicken or vegetable stock (pages 235, 233)	1.75 L
½ cup	grated Parmesan cheese	120 mL
½ tsp	freshly grated nutmeg	2.5 mL
¼ cup	whipping cream	60 mL
3 Tbsp	pumpkin seed oil	45 mL
2 Tbsp	toasted pumpkin seeds	30 mL
1 Tbsp	chopped chives	15 mL

This soup is very simple to make. Use unblemished squash that are heavy for their size, and if butternut squash are not available, try pumpkin. I grow winter squash in my garden and use it year-round: we fry the blossoms in the summer, then make soups with the flesh in the winter. Pumpkin seed oil is available at fine grocery stores; use hazelnut oil instead if you need to.

IN A LARGE saucepan fitted with a lid, heat the butter on medium heat. Add the shallots and sauté until lightly coloured, about 5 minutes. Add the squash and lightly season with salt and white pepper. Reduce the heat to low, cover and cook for 15 to 20 minutes, or until the squash is very soft.

Heat the chicken (or vegetable) stock in a medium pot on medium heat. Once the squash is very soft, pour enough hot stock over the squash to cover it by about 1 inch/2.5 cm. Simmer the squash mixture for 5 minutes, then add the Parmesan cheese and the nutmeg and cook for 2 minutes more. Remove the soup from the heat, transfer to a blender and pureé until smooth or use a handheld blender. Strain the soup through a fine-mesh sieve into a clean bowl and discard any solids. Stir in the cream and season with more salt, if necessary.

TO SERVE Pour the soup into 16 small espresso cups or ladle it into 6 bowls. Drizzle each serving with pumpkin seed oil, and top with pumpkin seeds and chives.

WINE Some of B.C.'s fine Pinot Blanc or a Mâconnais Chardonnay would complement this soup.

Roasted Beet Salad *with* Hazelnut Dressing *and* Beet Chips

Serves 4

ROASTED BEET SALAD

2 lbs	assorted baby and medium beets (such as purple, golden, Chioggia and white)	900 g
2 Tbsp	Golden Cariboo honey or similar unpasteurized honey	30 mL
¼ cup	water	60 mL
2 sprigs	fresh thyme	2 sprigs
2 cups	B.C. hothouse lettuces, washed and patted dry	480 mL

We serve this salad on our 100-mile tasting menu, a series of dishes made from products grown and raised within 160 kilometres/100 miles of the restaurant. Among the local ingredients we use are unpasteurized Golden Cariboo honey, a fireweed honey from Cariboo Apiaries in Lillooet; Bam!, a blackberry vinegar made by Wanda Dixon of Shady Glen Enterprises in West Vancouver, and hazelnut oil from Canadian Hazelnut in Agassiz. Salt is the only ingredient in this recipe that is not local.

In the winter we sometimes add a garnish of buffalo mozzarella and balsamic vinegar to replace the tomatoes we use in the summer. In either season, the roasted beets are really sweet.

ROASTED BEET SALAD Preheat the oven to 350°F/175°C. Cut 2 squares of aluminum foil, each 11 × 18 inches/ 30 × 45 cm, and place them one on top of the other on a clean work surface. Thoroughly wash the beets and mound them in the centre of the foil. Add the honey, water, thyme and a sprinkle of sea salt.

Fold the bottom and top edges of the foil over the beets, fold in the sides of the foil like an envelope and tightly roll the beets in the foil to make a package. Transfer to a baking sheet and bake for 35 to 45 minutes until the beets are very soft when a knife is inserted into them. Remove from the oven, unwrap the foil and allow the beets to cool slightly. Once they are cool enough to handle, rub them between your fingers to peel off the skins. Discard the foil and the skins, and set aside the beets until needed for the dressing and the finished dish.

continued overleaf...

HAZELNUT DRESSING Combine all of the ingredients in a blender and purée. Season with a little salt, if necessary. Will keep refrigerated in an airtight container for up to 3 days.

BEET CHIPS AND HAZELNUT TOPPING Thoroughly wash the beets, then use a mandoline to cut them as thinly as possible. Place the beets in a bowl of ice-cold water for 30 minutes.

In a small bowl, combine the hazelnuts and the hazelnut oil.

TO SERVE Divide the lettuces among 4 plates. Cut the roasted beets into various shapes according to their size and arrange an assortment over the lettuces. Drizzle the hazelnut dressing over the beets, spooning some hazelnuts on top, and garnish with the raw beet chips.

WINE A lighter red like village Beaujolais or Dolcetto would be nice, or opt for a contrasting, crisp Old World white like Spanish Verdejo or good-quality Italian Pinot Bianco.

HAZELNUT DRESSING

2 Tbsp	blackberry vinegar	30 mL
¼ cup	hazelnut oil	60 mL
¼ cup	diced cooked beets	60 mL
1 Tbsp	Golden Cariboo honey or similar unpasteurized honey	15 mL
2 Tbsp	hot water	30 mL

BEET CHIPS AND HAZELNUT TOPPING

2	medium beets (ideally 1 golden, 1 Chioggia)	2
2 Tbsp	B.C. hazelnuts, toasted and chopped	30 mL
2 Tbsp	hazelnut oil	30 mL

Rock Sole *with* Pemberton Potato Rösti *and* Lillooet Corn Sauce

Serves 4

SOLE

2	rock sole, each 2 lbs/900 g, skinned, filleted and bones reserved for the stock	2
2 Tbsp	clarified butter (page 232)	30 mL

FISH STOCK

2 Tbsp	butter	30 mL
1 stalk	celery, sliced	1 stalk
1	leek, white part only, sliced	1
2	shallots, sliced	2
1 clove	garlic, sliced	1 clove
	Bones from the sole, rinsed and chopped	
3 cups	water	750 mL

This is a plate that makes living on the West Coast easy. We really have it made out here: beautiful ocean, fertile farmland, great growing conditions, people who love food…and great skiing.

SOLE Portion each fillet into 2 or 3 pieces. Refrigerate until needed.

FISH STOCK Heat the butter in a medium saucepan on medium heat. Add the celery, leeks, shallots and garlic and sauté for 4 to 5 minutes to release the flavours. Do not colour the vegetables. Add the fish bones and the water and, with the heat still on medium, bring to almost a boil, then reduce the heat to low and simmer for 20 minutes, skimming the surface frequently with a spoon to remove any impurities. Strain the stock through a fine-mesh sieve into a clean bowl, discarding the solids, and set aside. Will keep refrigerated in an airtight container for up to 3 days.

CORN SAUCE In a medium saucepan fitted with a lid, heat the butter on low heat. Add the onions and chili peppers and sauté for 5 minutes. Increase the heat to medium, stir in the corn and white wine and cook until the wine has evaporated, about 5 minutes. Add the fish stock, cover and cook for 5 minutes. Remove the lid and continue cooking until most of the stock has reduced and the corn is tender, about 5 minutes. Add the bell peppers and the cream, lightly season with salt and set aside.

continued overleaf…

CORN SAUCE

2 Tbsp	butter	30 mL
1	small onion, minced	1
1	small chili pepper, seeded and minced	1
1½ cups	fresh corn kernels	355 mL
¼ cup	white wine	60 mL
1½ cups	reserved fish stock	375 mL
½	local red bell pepper, seeded and finely chopped	½
¼ cup	whipping cream	60 mL
1 Tbsp	roughly chopped parsley	15 mL
1 cup	mixed baby herbs and lettuces	240 mL

POTATO RÖSTI

2	large yellow-fleshed potatoes (such as Yukon Gold or Désirée), preferably from Pemberton	2
4 Tbsp	clarified butter (page 232)	60 mL

POTATO RÖSTI Peel the potatoes. Using a mandoline or a sharp knife, slice the potatoes into thin matchsticks. Place them in a bowl, season lightly with salt and pepper and allow them to stand 5 minutes to soften.

Heat a 5- to 6-inch/12.5- to 15-cm cast-iron or non-stick pan on high heat. Squeeze out any water from the potatoes and pour it off. Add 2 Tbsp/30 mL of the clarified butter and toss until the potatoes are well coated. Add the remaining butter to the pan, then add the potatoes. Using a spatula, press the potatoes to flatten them and reduce the heat to medium. Cook for 5 to 6 minutes until golden brown. Carefully flip the rösti, which should now look like a large potato pancake. Cook for 6 to 7 minutes more, or until crispy. Remove from the heat and keep warm.

FINISH SOLE Heat the clarified butter in a large sauté pan on medium-high heat. Season the sole fillets with salt and add half of the pieces to the pan. Pan-fry for 2 to 3 minutes, then turn the fish over and cook for 2 to 3 minutes more, keeping an eye on it as it cooks quite quickly. Transfer the fillets to a plate and pan-fry the second batch.

TO SERVE Place 2 spoonfuls of corn kernels onto the centre of each plate. Top with 2 to 3 pieces of the sole. Divide the remaining corn and its sauce among the plates. Cut the potato rösti into quarters and place a piece on each serving of sole. Sprinkle parsley over the sauce and garnish each plate with the mixed herbs and lettuces.

WINE Chardonnay is a natural pairing with the sole and the corn, and one from Argentina, Santa Barbara or Washington would be good here.

Roasted Pork Rack *with* Apple-Rosemary Sauce *and* Sunchoke Purée

Serves 4

The great thing about pork is that it is generally inexpensive compared with other meats. When buying pork, look for a good-quality organic meat because it will taste better and will generally have a bit more fat to keep it moist as it cooks. We get our pork from Sloping Hill Farm on Vancouver Island, which provides a particularly nice meat. Instead of the usual potatoes, we pair this pork with sunchokes. Also known as Jerusalem artichokes, they are best peeled in water to prevent discolouration. The applesauce in this recipe is a natural fit with pork and can be used with savoury or sweet dishes. We use Pink Lady, Granny Smith or Cox's Orange Pippin apple varieties. For a sweeter sauce, just add more honey.

ROASTED PORK Preheat the oven to 425°F/220°C. Place the pork rack on a clean work surface. Wrap one length of twine in the space between each rib, secure it in a knot, then cut off any excess twine.

Heat a large ovenproof sauté pan on high heat and add the clarified butter. Season the pork rack liberally with the salt. Add the pork to the pan, flesh side down, and sear until it is a deep golden brown, about 6 minutes. Remove from the heat. Turn the pork over, then place the sauté pan in the oven and roast for 10 minutes. Reduce the heat to 325°F/160°C. Remove the pork from the oven and pour off the excess fat. Lift the pork, add the thyme to the pan and place the pork on top of it, flesh side down. Roast for 30 minutes longer.

continued overleaf...

ROASTED PORK

1	fresh 4-bone rack of organic pork, total weight 3 lbs/ 1.4 kg, bones Frenched and chin bone removed	1
3 pieces	butcher's twine, each 8 inches/ 20 cm lengths	3 pieces
2 Tbsp	clarified butter (page 232)	30 mL
1 Tbsp	kosher salt	15 mL
2 sprigs	fresh thyme	2 sprigs
2 Tbsp	Golden Cariboo honey or similar unpasteurized honey	30 mL
1 cup	cooked globe carrots, warm, for garnish	240 mL

Remove the pork from the oven, and remove and discard the thyme. Using a pastry brush, baste the pork all over with the honey and return it to the oven, bone side down. Cook for 15 more minutes, or until a meat thermometer inserted in the centre of the pork reads 150°F/65°C. Baste the pork with the pan juices and allow it to rest for 10 to 15 minutes.

SUNCHOKE PURÉE Place the sunchokes in a saucepan, cover with the milk and add the thyme. Bring to a boil on medium heat, then reduce the heat to low and simmer for 15 to 20 minutes, until the sunchokes are very soft. Drain the sunchokes in a colander, discarding the cooking liquid and the thyme. Transfer the sunchokes to a blender, add the butter and purée until smooth. Season lightly with salt, then press the purée through a fine-mesh sieve and discard any solids. Set aside.

APPLE-ROSEMARY SAUCE In a medium saucepan fitted with a lid, combine the apples, honey, apple juice, rosemary and lemon thyme. Cook on medium heat until the apples start to soften and release their juices, about 8 minutes. Reduce the heat to low and cover the pot. Cook for 15 to 20 minutes, or until the apples are falling apart and quite soft. Remove from the heat, and discard the rosemary and lemon thyme sprigs. For a chunkier texture, mash the mixture with a fork or a potato masher. For a smoother sauce, transfer the mixture to a blender, purée and strain through a fine-mesh sieve. Return the sauce to a clean saucepan and keep warm on low heat.

TO SERVE Reheat the sunchoke purée in a saucepan on low heat. Divide the sunchoke purée among four warm plates. Slice the pork racks between the bones, discarding the butcher's twine, then position one piece of the pork on each plate. Top each serving of pork with 3 spoonfuls of the apple-rosemary sauce and garnish with carrots.

WINE A rich, full-bodied white such as Condrieu would be a fabulous pairing. Fine Burgundy of any colour also makes a natural match with the pork.

SUNCHOKE PURÉE

1 lb	sunchokes (about 12 to 14), peeled and sliced	455 g
3 cups	whole milk	750 mL
1 sprig	fresh thyme	1 sprig
1 Tbsp	unsalted butter	15 mL

APPLE-ROSEMARY SAUCE

4	large apples peeled, cored and cut into eighths	4
3 Tbsp	Golden Cariboo honey or similar unpasteurized liquid honey	45 mL
3 Tbsp	Denman Island apple juice or similar organic apple juice	45 mL
1 sprig	fresh rosemary	1 sprig
1 sprig	fresh lemon thyme	1 sprig

Roasted Pear *with* Lillooet Honey *and* Pear Sorbet

Serves 6

HONEY AND PEAR SORBET

4	ripe pears, preferably green or red Anjou	4
1½ cups	Denman Island apple juice or similar organic apple juice	375 mL
½ cup	Golden Cariboo honey or similar unpasteurized liquid honey	125 mL

ROASTED PEARS

1 cup	Golden Cariboo honey or similar unpasteurized honey	250 mL
¼ cup	Denman Island apple juice or similar organic apple juice	60 mL
6	ripe pears, preferably green or red Anjou	6
1 cup	B.C. hazelnuts, toasted, skinned and finely ground	240 mL

This is a dessert from our 100-mile tasting menu, which proves that you can make really nice desserts without using sugar and flour. The pears and apples we use in this recipe come from D'Arcy, a town just a few clicks past Pemberton. And the unpasteurized honey from the people at Cariboo Apiaries in Lillooet is outstanding.

HONEY AND PEAR SORBET Cut the pears in half and remove and discard the cores. Roughly chop the pears and place them in a medium pot. Add the apple juice and the honey and bring the mixture to a boil on high heat. Reduce the heat to medium and simmer, stirring frequently, until the pears are soft and completely broken down, 10 to 15 minutes. Remove the pot from the heat and allow the mixture to cool to room temperature, about 30 minutes.

Transfer the mixture to a blender and purée it, then strain it through a coarse-mesh sieve into a clean bowl. Refrigerate until cold, about 30 minutes. Pour the mixture into an ice cream machine and churn it according to the manufacturer's instructions. Will keep frozen in an airtight container for 3 to 4 days. Makes about 4 cups/1 L of sorbet.

ROASTED PEARS Preheat the oven to 375°F/190°C. Line a baking sheet with parchment paper. Gently heat the honey in a small saucepan on low heat and whisk in the apple juice. This will be the "basting" liquid for the pears. Remove the honey mixture from the heat.

Peel the pears, leaving the stems attached. Remove the core by scooping it out from the bottom of the fruit with a melon baller or a small spoon. Stand the pears upright on the baking sheet, then brush them with the honey mixture

and place the baking sheet in the oven. Bake the pears, basting them regularly with the honey mixture, until they are just tender when poked with a knife, 20 to 25 minutes. Remove the pears from the oven and allow them to cool. Reserve any leftover basting liquid.

TO SERVE Drizzle a spoonful of the honey basting liquid around each of 6 individual plates. Sprinkle a sixth of the hazelnuts on one side of each plate. Arrange a roasted pear next to the hazelnuts, standing it upright on the plate. Drizzle each pear with a bit of the basting liquid, then place a scoop of the sorbet on the bed of ground hazelnuts. Serve immediately.

WINE A Hungarian Tokaji Aszú of 5 or 6 puttonyos is worth the search, or pair the fruit and honey flavours with a late-harvest B.C. dessert white.

WINTER
recipes

Winter

WINTER, MORE than any other season, is synonymous with Whistler. Visitors come from around the world to test their mettle on the mountains' 1,500-metre (5,000-foot) vertical drops, to carve through knee-deep powder on one of hundreds of trails or just to ride the gondolas and gaze across the valley at spectacular crevassed glaciers. Locals, including the staff at Araxi, are equally awed: "I absolutely love Whistler, the lifestyle. I mean, skiing fresh powder on the slopes in the morning, off to work in the afternoon—what could be more ideal?" exclaims sous-chef Tim Pickwell. When the sun shines, the snow sparkles and the slopes are all sugar, the village has the feel of a giant winter party. At the restaurant, the excitement is palpable—the room is prepared and the team is poised for the evening's service.

Even when snow blankets the mountains and the farms in the winter months, there are lots of local ingredients available. Cold coastal waters nurture sweet and briny Dungeness crabs, and stunning varieties of clams and mussels await gathering at the shellfish farms on Quadra and Saltspring Islands. A live tank at the restaurant ensures that the crustaceans remain fresh from ocean to plate. Duck, lamb, caribou and beef are in ready supply, as are cellared root crops and the summer-ripe fruit stored at the peak of perfection.

Executive chef James Walt knows how to build a plate, and how textures and flavours interact to make a whole. Winter dishes are focused and precise, and they often play on one key element.

James explains, "In the winter, we slow cook and roast more items. Root vegetables and cellared crops are cooked longer to capture their brilliant flavours." Highlights of the winter menu include golden mussels with salsify, leeks and an apple dressing that accentuates the fresh shellfish, and crab and coconut milk soup. Braised beef short ribs are served with pickled mushrooms, duck confit with lentils and honey-roasted carrots.

The winter menus at Araxi hold some surprises—a selection of little-known but local, seasonal ingredients, including nutty crosnes, sweet and pungent Music garlic, crunchy red and white sunchokes and buttery Désirée, True Blue or Sieglinde potatoes. Winter dishes retain the ingredient-driven focus that is the hallmark of Araxi's menus and a legacy of James's time in Rome as the chef to the Canadian ambassador in Italy. "I like Italian sensibilities in cooking," he says, "especially the idea of taking one product and layering it with complementary flavours: a silky polenta, for

example, served with peppery winter greens and a slightly salty, rich and creamy fonduta."

Like James, pastry chef Aaron Heath focuses on local flavours during the winter, including pears, apples and dried fruits. Often he pairs these with chocolate, making a bold statement with Araxi's legendary molten chocolate cakes or simple pots de crème. Beautiful buttery brioches complement sweet and savoury preparations, and occasionally pineapples or lemons are baked into a smooth and zesty tart to evoke the memory of summer. "At this time of year, the combination of creamy mascarpone cheesecake with tangy Pink Lady apples makes perfect sense to me," states Aaron.

When the sun sets and the gondolas stop running, Whistler's famous nightlife is just beginning. Visitors criss-cross the main square bundled in scarves and swaddled in down jackets against the evening cold. The lights on the ski slopes glow against the inky sky. At Araxi, the shellfish are on ice, the wine is breathing and the evening is young. It is the perfect time to sit back, relive the day and savour the best that Whistler has to offer.

APPETIZERS AND CANAPÉS

ENTREES

Fresh Noodles *with* Manila Clams, Swiss Chard *and* Kale   180

Saddle *of* Rabbit *with* Buttered Noodles, Carrots *and* Mustard Sauce   182

Crispy Duck Confit *with* Lentils *and* Honey-roasted Carrots   186

Braised Beef Short Ribs with Cauliflower
Purée *and* Pickled Mushrooms   189

Pepper-crusted Rib-eye Steaks *with*
Wild Mushroom Ragout *and* Roasted Baby Beets   192

Veal Sweetbreads *with* Pomme Purée,
Brussels Sprouts *and* Persillade   195

Roasted Rack *of* Lamb *with* Spaetzle *and* Parsley Roots   199

Roasted Portobello Mushrooms *with* Chickpea
Fritters *and* Cucumber Yogurt   202

Parmesan Polenta *with* Braised Greens *and* Fonduta   205

DESSERTS

Molten Chocolate Cakes *with* Crème Anglaise   208

Lemon Tart   210

Pineapple Upside-down "Tart"   213

Black Forest Cake *with* Brandied-Cherry Ice Cream   216

Chocolate Caramel Pots de Crème *with*
Milk Chocolate–Almond Biscotti   221

Mascarpone Cheesecake *with* Honey-
Caramel Apples *and* Almond Praline   226

Fingerling Potato Chips *and* Pecorino-Chive Cream

Serves 4 as an amuse-bouche (Yields 2 cups/480 mL)

POTATO CHIPS

8 oz	large fingerling potatoes (about 7 to 8)	225 g
12 cups	peanut or vegetable oil, for deep-frying	3 L
1 Tbsp	fleur de sel	15 mL
1 Tbsp	chives, cut in 1-inch/2.5 cm sticks, for garnish	15 mL
2 to 3	fresh bay leaves, for garnish	2 to 3

PECORINO-CHIVE CREAM

1⅔ cups	whipping cream	415 mL
1 clove	garlic, sliced	1 clove
1	bay leaf	1
1 sprig	fresh rosemary	1 sprig
⅞ cup	grated pecorino Romano cheese	210 mL
3½ oz	goat cheese	100 g
2 Tbsp	chopped chives	30 mL

At the restaurant, we sometimes serve these "chips and dip" as an amuse-bouche when guests arrive. There is something comforting about the familiar potato chip, and pecorino Romano is a favourite of mine—I like the saltiness of the cheese and its hayfield smell.

POTATO CHIPS Rinse and scrub the potatoes. Using a mandoline, slice the potatoes as thinly as possible. Do not allow the slices to break. Place the potatoes in a large bowl, cover with cold water and refrigerate for at least 12 hours.

PECORINO-CHIVE CREAM Place the cream, garlic, bay leaf and rosemary in a small pot on medium heat. Once the cream is hot, remove from the heat and allow it to infuse for 20 minutes.

Combine the pecorino Romano and goat cheeses in a medium bowl. Warm the cream infusion on low heat, then strain it through a fine-mesh sieve over the cheeses. Discard the solids, then whisk the cream and cheese mixture until smooth. Fold in the chopped chives and refrigerate the dip for 2 hours, or until it becomes firm.

FINISH POTATO CHIPS Fill a deep pot or a wok two-thirds full with peanut (or vegetable) oil and heat it to 330°F/165°C (use a deep-fat thermometer to check the temperature). Drain the potatoes and carefully pat them dry with paper towels. Fry the potatoes in small batches for 3 minutes, until golden brown, then use a slotted spoon to transfer the chips to paper towels and season with fleur de sel.

TO SERVE Spoon the pecorino-chive cream into a piping bag fitted with a wide nozzle. Pipe a line of dip along each chip. Arrange the potato chips on a serving platter, garnish with the chive sticks and bay leaves and pass the plate around.

WINE Sip village Chablis or unoaked B.C. Chardonnay, or some B.C. bubbly would be fun.

Dungeness Crab *and* Coconut-Milk Soup

Serves 10 to 12 (Yields 12 cups/3 L)

10 cups	fish or chicken stock (pages 233, 235)	2.5 L
1	live Dungeness crab, about 2 lbs/900 g	1
2 Tbsp	grapeseed oil	30 mL
2	medium onions, minced	2
½-inch piece	ginger, peeled and minced	1-cm piece
2	red jalapeño peppers, seeded and minced	2
1½ Tbsp	mild curry powder	25 mL
1 Tbsp	ground turmeric	15 mL
2½ cups	coconut milk	625 mL
	Juice of 2 limes	
2 Tbsp	chopped fresh cilantro leaves or chives	30 mL

I like subtle ethnic flavours in some dishes, such as this soup in which the curry sets off but doesn't overwhelm the flavour of the crab. At the restaurant, we sometimes serve a crab spring roll to dip in this soup. The recipe works with lobster as well: just cook the lobster for 8 minutes in the stock and make the rest of the dish the same way you would with the crab. Chilling the live shellfish in the freezer for 20 to 30 minutes before you begin makes it easier to handle.

IN A LARGE pot fitted with a lid, bring the fish (or chicken) stock to a boil on high heat. Add the crab, reduce the heat to medium, cover and cook for 12 minutes. Using tongs, transfer the crab to a large bowl, placing it shell side down, and refrigerate for 30 minutes or until chilled. Strain the stock through a fine-mesh sieve, discard the solids and set aside.

Heat the grapeseed oil in a medium saucepan on medium-low heat, then add the onions, ginger and jalapeño peppers and sauté until very soft and fragrant, about 10 minutes. Add the curry powder and turmeric and cook 3 minutes more to release the flavours. Add the strained stock and the coconut milk, increase the heat to medium-high and bring to a boil. Reduce the heat to low and simmer for 15 to 20 minutes. Remove from the heat, stir in the lime juice and season with salt. Set aside.

To clean the crab, hold the base of the crab with one hand and lift off the shell with the other hand. Discard the shell. With a spoon, gently scrape away and discard the gills on either side (the off-white bits between the legs), the intestine and the other innards that run down the back and fill the cavity. Rinse the crab under cold water. Break the body in half and twist off the legs. Using a nutcracker

or a mallet, crack the legs. Remove the meat with a fork or a pick, then crack the body sections and remove the meat from those as well.

TO SERVE Heat the soup on medium heat, then add the crabmeat. Garnish with the cilantro (or chives) and ladle into warmed bowls.

WINE An Alsatian blend like Joie's Noble Blend is a natural B.C. pairing, or enjoy some Mosel Riesling.

Red *and* Yellow Endive Salad
with Walnuts, Pears *and* Blue Cheese

Serves 4

Moonstruck Organic Cheese on Saltspring Island makes a blue cheese called Blossom's Blue that works well for this salad. If you cannot find it, use a mild creamy blue cheese like Cambozola instead. Also be sure to use ripe pears, as they become much sweeter as they soften. Try braising endives, just like the artichokes on page 52, for an interesting side dish with this salad.

HONEY-MUSTARD VINAIGRETTE In a small bowl, combine the grainy mustard and the honey. In another small bowl, whisk together the walnut and grapeseed oils. Whisk the white wine vinegar into the honey mustard, then slowly whisk the combined oils into the honey-mustard mixture. Season lightly with salt. Will keep refrigerated in an airtight container for up to 7 days.

ENDIVE SALAD Cut the endives in half lengthwise. Discard the bottoms and the cores. Slice the endives again lengthwise into quarters, then rinse them under cold water to crisp the leaves. Pat them dry with paper towels.

Wash the pears and cut them in half. Discard the cores, then thinly slice the pears. Place the pears, endives and cheese in a medium bowl.

TO SERVE Add the walnuts to the salad and toss with a third of the vinaigrette. Divide the salad among 4 bowls and drizzle with additional vinaigrette. Garnish with the basil.

WINE Vintage Champagne holds up to the complex flavours of this salad.

HONEY-MUSTARD VINAIGRETTE

1 Tbsp	grainy mustard	15 mL
1 Tbsp	honey	15 mL
3 Tbsp	walnut oil	45 mL
½ cup	grapeseed oil	125 mL
3 Tbsp	white wine vinegar	45 mL

ENDIVE SALAD

2 heads	white Belgian endive	2 heads
2 heads	red Belgian endive	2 heads
2	ripe pears	2
3 ½ oz	blue cheese, crumbled	100 g
½ cup	whole walnuts, toasted	120 mL
½ cup	baby basil leaves in bunches	120 mL

Golden Mussels *with* Pickled Salsify, Leeks *and* Apple Vinaigrette

Serves 4

LEEKS AND PICKLED SALSIFY

3 cups	vegetable stock (page 233)	750 mL
3 Tbsp	olive oil	45 mL
2 cloves	garlic, sliced	2 cloves
2	leeks, white and light green parts only	2
1½ cups	sweet pickling brine (page 232)	375 mL
2	salsify roots	2
6	fresh chives, cut in 2-inch/5-cm lengths, for garnish	6

MUSSELS

2 Tbsp	olive oil	30 mL
3	shallots, thinly sliced	3
1½ lbs	farmed golden mussels, washed and debearded	680 g
1	bay leaf	1
⅓ cup	white wine	80 mL

There is something sophisticated about shellfish served out of the shell. Here, we pair mussels with tender leeks that go well with the sweetness of apples. Be sure to cook the leeks until they are tender; you can cut into the bulb end while they are cooking to check if they are soft. The pickled salsify—a European root vegetable with a mild flavour—makes a really interesting addition to a green salad as well. If you cannot find salsify, use carrots or parsnips instead. For an elegant presentation, garnish this dish with apple chips (page 240).

LEEKS AND PICKLED SALSIFY Bring the vegetable stock, olive oil and garlic to a boil in a medium saucepan on high heat. Cut the leeks in half and add them to the liquid. Reduce the heat to low and simmer the leeks until they are very tender, 30 to 40 minutes. Remove the pot from the heat and allow the leeks to cool in the cooking liquid.

Heat the pickling brine in a medium saucepan on medium heat until hot. Remove from the heat and set aside. Peel and discard the dark skin from the salsify. Using a vegetable peeler, shave the salsify into thin strips and add it to the hot pickling brine. Allow the salsify to stand in the brine as it cools.

MUSSELS In a medium saucepan fitted with a lid, heat the olive oil on low heat. Add the shallots and cook them for 2 minutes to release the flavours. Add the mussels and bay leaf, increase the heat to high, then add the white wine and cover. Cook the mussels for 3 minutes, then use a slotted spoon to transfer them to a bowl as they open. Discard

continued overleaf...

APPLE VINAIGRETTE

1	Pink Lady or Granny Smith apple	1
1 Tbsp	Dijon mustard	15 mL
1 Tbsp	brown sugar	15 mL
1 Tbsp	white wine vinegar	15 mL
3 Tbsp	reserved mussel jus	45 mL
⅔ cup	grapeseed oil	165 mL

any mussels that do not open. Strain the cooking liquid through a fine-mesh sieve into a small pot on medium heat, discarding any solids, and reduce by half, about 8 minutes. Refrigerate this mussel jus for 30 minutes, until chilled, then reserve for the vinaigrette. Remove and discard the mussel shells, then refrigerate the mussels for 30 minutes, until chilled.

APPLE VINAIGRETTE Peel, core and roughly chop the apple, then purée it with the Dijon mustard and brown sugar in a blender at high speed, adding the white wine vinegar and the mussel jus. Scrape down the sides of the blender. With the motor running at medium speed, add the grapeseed oil and process until all of the ingredients are well incorporated.

TO SERVE Drain the leeks and cut them in half lengthwise, trimming the bottoms and removing any sand at either end. Place the leeks in a bowl and toss them with 3 Tbsp/45 mL of the vinaigrette. Divide the leeks among 4 plates, then top each serving with a quarter of the chilled mussels. Dress the mussels with 2 spoonfuls of the vinaigrette. Drain the salsify, then garnish each plate with chives and pieces of salsify.

WINE Try B.C. or Oregon Pinot Gris, or unoaked or lightly oaked Chardonnay from these regions.

Moonstruck Cheese Soufflé *with* Frisée *and* Toasted Almonds

Serves 6

Andrew Richardson, a former chef at Araxi, really perfected this soufflé. We use Moonstruck's White Grace cheese in this recipe, but an aged white Cheddar would be a good substitute. You can add a little crabmeat to it or some blanched spinach. Or try adding different flavours to the cream, or tiny garnishes like roasted figs or baked apples.

CHEESE SOUFFLÉS Lightly butter the bottom and sides of six 4-inch/10-cm ramekins with the softened butter, then sprinkle them with ¼ cup/60 mL of the finely grated Parmesan cheese, rolling the ramekins to ensure the cheese coats the sides as well. Set aside.

In a medium saucepan, bring the milk, onions, bay leaf and cloves to a boil on high heat. Turn off the heat and allow the mixture to infuse for 20 minutes.

Preheat the oven to 375°F/190°C. Melt the unsalted butter in another medium pot, then whisk in the flour to form a roux. Reduce the heat to very low and cook for 5 minutes.

Strain the infused milk mixture through a fine-mesh sieve into a clean bowl. Discard any solids. Slowly pour the milk mixture into the roux, whisking constantly to prevent lumps. Increase the heat to medium-low and cook for 5 minutes, until the sauce has thickened. Remove from the heat and add the Moonstruck cheese and the salt, whisking until the cheese has melted. Transfer this cheese mixture to a large bowl.

continued overleaf...

CHEESE SOUFFLÉS

2 Tbsp	butter, softened	30 mL
½ cup	finely grated Parmesan cheese	120 mL
1¾ cups	whole milk	435 mL
½	onion, sliced	½
1	bay leaf	1
2	whole cloves	2
¼ cup	unsalted butter	60 mL
¼ cup	all-purpose flour	60 mL
¾ cup	Moonstruck White Grace cheese, grated	180 mL
1 tsp	kosher salt	5 mL
6	egg whites	6
6	egg yolks	6
¾ cup	whipping cream	185 mL
1 sprig	fresh thyme	1 sprig
2 Tbsp	sour cream	30 mL
1 Tbsp	chopped fresh chives	15 mL

In the bowl of a mixer fitted with a whisk attachment, whip the egg whites on medium speed until they form soft peaks and just start to hold their shape, about 5 minutes.

Add the egg yolks to the cheese mixture, whisking them in until they are well incorporated. Using a spatula, add a third of the whipped egg whites to the cheese mixture and blend until combined, then fold in the remainder of the egg whites until just combined.

Fill the ramekins three-quarters full with the cheese mixture and place them in a deep baking dish. Pour very hot tap water into the baking dish until it reaches halfway up the sides of the ramekins. Bake in the oven for 12 minutes. Turn the baking dish around and cook for 8 to 10 minutes longer, or until the soufflés are golden brown and fluffed. Remove from the oven and allow to stand for 3 minutes, then remove the ramekins from the water. Allow the ramekins to stand for 2 to 3 minutes more. Using a small spatula or a paring knife, unmould the soufflés and place them on parchment paper or refrigerate them until cool.

FRISÉE SALAD In a bowl, combine the frisée lettuce and the chervil and dress with the vinaigrette.

FINISH SOUFFLÉS In a small saucepan, bring the whipping cream and thyme to a boil on medium heat. Reduce the heat to low and simmer gently for 5 minutes. Remove from the heat and whisk in the sour cream and the remaining ¼ cup/60 mL of grated Parmesan cheese. Strain this mixture through a fine-mesh sieve into a clean bowl.

Preheat the oven to 350°F/175°C. Place the unmoulded soufflés on a baking sheet and cook for 7 minutes, or until they again fluff up and turn light golden brown.

TO SERVE Place a soufflé on each plate. Add the chives to the warm cream sauce, then divide this mixture over the soufflés. Top with a serving of the frisée salad and garnish with toasted almonds. Serve immediately.

WINE Complement the rich flavours of this dish with Meursault or Russian River Chardonnay, or highlight the light texture with some Champagne.

FRISÉE SALAD

1 ½ cups	frisée lettuce, light green and white parts only	355 mL
¼ cup	fresh chervil leaves	60 mL
2 Tbsp	basic vinaigrette (page 236)	30 mL
3 Tbsp	sliced almonds, toasted, for garnish	45 mL

Wild Mushroom Consommé *with* Herb Crepes

Serves 10 to 12

MUSHROOM CONSOMMÉ

1	whole chicken, about 4 lbs/1.8kg, bones and skin removed	1
2	large carrots	2
2 stalks	celery	2 stalks
1-inch piece	fresh ginger, peeled	2.5-cm piece
8	king oyster mushrooms	8
1 cup	dried shiitake mushrooms, soaked to rehydrate	240 mL
1 sprig	fresh thyme	1 sprig
1 sprig	fresh parsley	1 sprig
5	egg whites	5
16 cups	chicken stock (page 235)	4 L
¼ cup	soy sauce	60 mL
½ cup	Madeira wine	125 mL
2 Tbsp	sliced green onions, for garnish	30 mL
½ cup	enoki mushrooms, for garnish	120 mL

I would usually use a dark or roasted stock to make a consommé, but a light stock works well here. When you are making crepes, cook some extra ones, as they store well. You can stuff and bake them for a main course or fill them with fruit and whipped cream for dessert. Dried mushrooms pack a punch; after soaking them, reserve the liquid to make cream sauces or soups.

MUSHROOM CONSOMMÉ In a food processor or using a mixer fitted with a grinder attachment, finely grind together the chicken, carrots, celery, ginger, oyster and shiitake mushrooms, thyme and parsley. Transfer the chicken mixture to a large bowl and add the egg whites, stirring until well combined. Cover and refrigerate for 45 minutes, until chilled.

Place the chilled chicken mixture in a heavy-bottomed saucepan, then add the chicken stock and stir to combine. Heat on medium-low heat for 15 to 20 minutes, stirring every 5 minutes to prevent the mixture from sticking to the bottom of the pot.

Once the chicken and vegetables float to the surface and begin to form a raft, stop stirring and allow it to form. The raft will clarify the stock and add flavour. Reduce the heat to low and allow the soup to simmer for 35 to 45 minutes. Pour in the soy sauce, but do not stir.

Pour the Madeira wine into a small pot. Place the pan on medium heat, stand away from the stove and use a barbecue lighter or a long fireplace match to light the fumes at the edge of the pan. (Be careful to keep your hair and any loose clothing away from the pot, as the flames will rush up.) Allow the flames to burn for 2 minutes. If necessary, cover with a lid to put out the flames. Add this flambéed

continued overleaf...

CREPES

1 cup	whole milk	250 mL
2	eggs	2
1 cup	all-purpose flour	240 mL
½ tsp	salt	2.5 mL
2 Tbsp	melted unsalted butter	30 mL
2 Tbsp	chopped fresh parsley or chervil	30 mL
1 tsp	vegetable oil	5 mL

wine to the soup, then lightly season the soup with salt and remove from the heat.

Line a fine-mesh sieve with cheesecloth and set it over a clean pot. Using a ladle, carefully spoon the broth from the pot into the cheesecloth-lined sieve. Don't agitate the raft too much or the consommé will become cloudy. Discard the solids and set aside the consommé.

CREPES In a medium bowl, whisk together the milk and the eggs. Slowly add the flour, whisking constantly to prevent lumps from forming. Pass the batter through a fine-mesh sieve, discarding any solids, then mix in the salt, melted butter and parsley (or chervil). Allow the batter to stand for 15 minutes.

Heat a non-stick crepe pan or a small sauté pan on medium-low heat. Drizzle the oil on a paper towel, then quickly wipe the pan with it. Drop 2 Tbsp/30 mL of the batter onto the pan, then tilt the pan so the batter coats the bottom. Cook for about 2 minutes, or until the crepe has set and the edges start to brown. Using a large spatula, flip the crepe and cook for 1 to 2 minutes more. Transfer the cooked crepe to a warm plate and repeat with the remaining batter. You should end up with about 12 crepes.

Roll the crepes into individual logs like jelly rolls, then slice them into thin spirals.

TO SERVE Warm the individual soup bowls. Heat the consommé on medium heat until it is hot. Divide the crepe spirals among the warmed bowls, then garnish with green onions and enoki mushrooms. Ladle the consommé into the bowls and serve immediately.

WINE A little sip of amontillado sherry would be nice with the consommé.

Seared Scallops *with* White Bean Purée *and* Bacon

Serves 4

Scallops are one of my favourite foods to work with, which is probably why they appear in this book a few times. Any leftover bean purée can be used as a dip for bread; just drizzle lots of good olive oil on it.

BEAN PURÉE On the cheesecloth, place the thyme, rosemary, bay leaf and peppercorns. Gather the edges of the cheesecloth and tie them together tightly with kitchen twine to make a bouquet garni.

Rinse the beans and place them in a large saucepan with the carrots, onion, leeks, celery, bacon (or salt pork) and the bouquet garni. Cover with enough vegetable stock (or water) to reach 2 inches/5 cm above the beans and bring to a boil on medium heat. Reduce the heat to medium-low and simmer gently, skimming impurities off the surface, for about 1 hour or until the beans become soft. Season with salt and continue cooking until very tender, about 20 minutes more.

Drain the beans and vegetables, reserving 1½ cups/ 375 mL of the cooking liquid. Discard the bacon, vegetables and bouquet garni. Place the beans and the reserved cooking liquid in a food processor or a blender and purée at high speed until smooth. Pass the bean purée through a fine-mesh sieve into a bowl, discarding any solids.

continued overleaf…

BEAN PURÉE

3-inch square	cheesecloth	7.5-cm square
2 sprigs	fresh thyme	2 sprigs
1 sprig	fresh rosemary	1 sprig
1	bay leaf	1
10	black peppercorns	10
3 cups	navy or cannellini beans, soaked overnight in cold water and drained	720 mL
1	carrot, halved	1
1	onion, peeled only	1
1	leek, tops removed, halved	1
2 stalks	celery, halved	2 stalks
2 oz	bacon or salt pork, whole piece (about 4 to 5 thick slices)	60 g
8 to 10 cups	vegetable stock (page 233) or water	2 to 2.5 L

SEARED SCALLOPS Preheat the oven to 350°F/175°C. Line a baking sheet with parchment paper. Arrange the bacon on the parchment paper, then cover it with another sheet of parchment paper. Place a second baking sheet on top. Bake for 12 minutes or until crisp. (Check on it after 8 minutes to make sure it isn't cooking too quickly.) Remove from the oven and allow to cool.

In a small bowl, combine the curry powder and salt. Heat the clarified butter in a sauté pan on high heat. Season the scallops with the curry salt and place them in the pan. Sauté for 2 minutes until nicely browned on one side, then turn the scallops over and baste them with the butter. Cook for 1 more minute and then remove them from the pan.

TO SERVE Spoon a line of bean purée onto each plate. Top the purée with 3 scallops and the 2 slices of bacon. Garnish each plate with a quarter of the micro greens and drizzle with the vinaigrette.

WINE Pair this dish with Pouilly-Fumé, California Fumé Blanc or B.C. white Meritage, or enjoy it with Austrian Grüner Veltliner.

SEARED SCALLOPS

8 very thin slices	bacon	8 very thin slices
¼ tsp	curry powder	1 mL
¾ tsp	salt	4 mL
2 Tbsp	clarified butter (page 232)	30 mL
12	medium fresh scallops	12
½ cup	micro greens	120 mL
3 Tbsp	basic vinaigrette (page 236)	45 mL

Foie Gras *and* Chicken Liver Parfait *with* Onion Compote *and* Brioche

Serves 18 to 20

FOIE GRAS AND CHICKEN LIVER PARFAIT

1 cup	port	250 mL
⅔ cup	brandy	165 mL
6	shallots, sliced	6
2 cloves	garlic, sliced	2 cloves
1 sprig	fresh thyme	1 sprig
10 oz	fresh chicken livers	285 g
9 oz	foie gras	255 g
4 cups	whole milk	1 L
¾ tsp	pink salt or ½ tsp/2.5 mL table salt	4 mL
1 tsp	kosher salt	5 mL
6	eggs, at room temperature	6
1¼ lbs	unsalted butter, melted, at room temperature	550 g
1 loaf	brioche (page 242)	1 loaf

This classic parfait is good in any season and although it is a little costly to make, this recipe yields a lot and leftovers can be stored for up to 1 week. At the restaurant, we lightly coat the parfait with soft butter before serving to stop it from oxidizing on the outside.

FOIE GRAS AND CHICKEN LIVER PARFAIT Combine the port, brandy, shallots, garlic and thyme in a medium saucepan on medium heat. Reduce until all of the alcohol evaporates and the mixture becomes like syrup, about 10 minutes. Discard the thyme sprig.

Roughly chop the chicken livers and slice the foie gras, then place them in a large bowl and add the milk. Set this mixture aside until it reaches room temperature, about 25 minutes.

Preheat the oven to 300°F/150°C. Drain and discard the milk, then season the chicken livers and foie gras with the pink (or table) salt and the kosher salt. Transfer the mixture to a blender or a food processor, add the reduced shallot mixture and purée at high speed until smooth. With the motor running at high speed, slowly add the eggs to the liver mixture. Once they are incorporated, slowly add the melted butter. Press the purée through a fine-mesh sieve into a 3 inch × 12 inch × 3 inch/7.5 cm × 30 cm × 7.5 cm terrine mould and cover tightly with aluminum foil. Place the terrine mould in a roasting pan and pour enough hot water into the pan to reach halfway up the sides of the mould. Put the roasting pan in the oven and bake for 1 hour and 10 minutes.

continued overleaf...

2	red onions, sliced	2
1	small white onion, sliced	1
	Juice and zest of 1 orange	
	Juice and zest of 1 lemon	
¼ cup	brown sugar	60 mL
½ cup	red wine vinegar	125 mL
1 stick	cinnamon	1 stick
	Small pinch of red chili flakes	

Remove the foil and jiggle the mould; the loaf will be soft but set and slightly fluffy. Remove the terrine mould from the water bath. Cover and refrigerate for 24 hours.

To unmould the terrine, fill the same roasting pan with very hot water. Place the cold terrine in the water and allow it to stand for 3 minutes. Run a paring or a palette knife along the sides of the terrine, then cover it with a serving plate or a board and gently invert the mould and the plate (or board) together. The parfait should slide out. Repeat, if necessary. Use a spatula or a palette knife to smooth the sides of the unmoulded terrine. Refrigerate for 45 minutes, until chilled.

ONION COMPOTE In a medium saucepan fitted with a lid, combine all the ingredients and bring to a simmer, uncovered, on medium heat. Reduce the heat to low and cover. Cook, checking and stirring frequently to prevent sticking, until the onions are very soft, 1½ to 2 hours. Remove from the heat and refrigerate for 45 minutes, until chilled.

Transfer the onion mixture to a clean work surface and chop it to obtain a smooth texture. Makes about 2 cups/500 mL of onion compote. Will keep refrigerated in an airtight container for up to 7 days.

TO SERVE Slice and toast the brioche. Run a sharp knife under hot water, then slice the parfait into ¼-inch/5-mm pieces. Place a slice of the parfait on each plate, and top with a spoonful of the chilled compote. Serve the toasted brioche on the side.

WINE Sauternes is fabulous with the pâté, or try other "stickies" such as Monbazillac or Muscat de Beaumes-de-Venise. I also pair this dish with young, fruit-forward, tannic reds for something different.

Sweet Onion Soup *with* Aged Cheddar *and* Gruyère

Serves 4 to 6 (Yields 10 cups/2.5 L)

Araxi is located at a ski resort, so you can guess that this soup is a huge seller at the restaurant. Make sure that you cook the onions deeply to develop their flavour. Maple syrup and Quebec cheddar make this a uniquely Canadian dish. Depending on how much cheese you like, feel free to vary the quantities in the topping.

ONION SOUP On the cheesecloth, place the thyme, rosemary, parsley, bay leaf and peppercorns. Gather the edges of the cheesecloth and tie them together tightly with kitchen twine to make a bouquet garni.

In a large pot, heat the butter on medium heat. Add the onions and the bouquet garni and cook until the onions start to caramelize, about 15 minutes. Reduce the heat to low and cook, stirring frequently, until the onions are a deep brown, about 30 minutes. Pour in the sherry and cook for another 5 minutes, until the sherry is evaporated.

In a medium bowl, combine the veal and chicken stocks. Stir 2 cups/500 mL of the combined stocks into the onion soup and allow it to reduce slightly, about 10 minutes. Add the remaining stock and simmer for 15 minutes, then add the maple syrup and season with salt and pepper. Discard the bouquet garni. Will keep refrigerated in an airtight container for up to 5 days.

CHEESE TOPPING Preheat the oven to 375°F/190°C. Arrange the bread slices on a baking sheet and toast them until they are golden brown on both sides, 8 to 10 minutes.

In a small bowl, combine the Gruyère and cheddar cheeses.

continued overleaf...

ONION SOUP

3-inch square	cheesecloth	7.5-cm square
3 sprigs	fresh thyme	3 sprigs
1 sprig	fresh rosemary	1 sprig
2 sprigs	fresh parsley	2 sprigs
1	bay leaf	1
10	black peppercorns	10
⅜ cup	unsalted butter	90 mL
5 lbs	onions, thinly sliced	2.25 kg
1 cup	sherry	250 mL
4 cups	veal stock (page 234)	1 L
6 cups	chicken stock (page 235)	1.5 L
¼ cup	maple syrup	60 mL

CHEESE TOPPING

1 loaf	day-old bread, preferably sourdough, in ¼-inch/5-mm slices	1 loaf
1 cup	grated Gruyère cheese	240 mL
1 cup	grated aged Quebec cheddar cheese	240 mL

TO SERVE Preheat the broiler. Divide the hot soup into individual French onion soup bowls or deep ovenproof soup bowls set on a baking sheet. Arrange 3 slices of toasted bread on top of each serving and generously cover with the mixed cheeses. Place the sheet in the middle of the oven and broil until the cheeses are bubbling and brown, about 4 minutes. Serve immediately.

WINE B.C. or Alsace Gewürztraminer is a surprisingly delicious match.

Albacore Tuna Sashimi *with* Citrus-Soy Dressing *and* Cucumber Pearls

Serves 4

When serving this tuna dish, be sure the fish is very cold. The shiso leaves, which taste like cumin, have a cooling effect as well and freshen your taste buds. And the more you rinse the daikon, the more the sharp radish taste dissipates and the crunchier it becomes. The technique for making the cucumber pearls also works with carrot or beet juice.

SASHIMI Place the daikon in a bowl of ice-cold water and allow to stand for 20 minutes. Drain, then repeat twice with fresh ice water to crisp the daikon and soften the flavour. Refrigerate until needed.

CUCUMBER PEARLS Pour the vegetable oil into a glass bowl and refrigerate for 2 hours.

Run the cucumber through a juicer or purée it in a blender and press it through a fine-mesh sieve into a clean bowl. Reserve 1 cup/250 mL of the juice. Discard any solids and any extra juice.

Pour ½ cup/125 mL cold water into a small bowl, then add the gelatin leaves and allow them to soften for 3 minutes. If using granulated gelatin, sprinkle it onto the cold water and allow to soften for 3 minutes.

In a small saucepan, heat a quarter of the cucumber juice, the red wine gastrique and the salt on low heat for 2 minutes. Remove from the heat, add the gelatin and stir to dissolve. Add the remaining cucumber juice and refrigerate the mixture for 10 minutes to allow it to cool slightly.

continued overleaf...

SASHIMI

1 cup	daikon radish, sliced into thin matchsticks	240 mL
12-oz piece	sashimi-grade albacore tuna	340-g piece
8	shiso leaves	8
½ cup	citrus-soy dressing (page 237)	125 mL

CUCUMBER PEARLS

2 cups	vegetable oil	500 mL
2	English cucumbers, halved and seeded	2
4 leaves	gelatin	4 leaves
	OR	
¼ oz	granulated gelatin	8 g
1 Tbsp	red wine gastrique (page 45)	15 mL
¼ tsp	kosher salt	1 mL

Transfer the juice mixture to a squeeze bottle (or use a spoon) and, working quickly, drip many small drops into the chilled oil. The drops will set into little balls. Strain the mixture through a fine-mesh sieve. (The oil can be saved to make salad dressing.) The pearls will keep refrigerated in an airtight container for up to 2 days.

TO SERVE Divide the daikon among 4 bowls. Thinly slice the tuna into 12 pieces. Arrange 3 slices of tuna over the daikon in each bowl, then garnish with 2 shiso leaves and a spoonful of cucumber pearls. Serve the citrus-soy dressing in individual dipping bowls on the side.

WINE New Zealand Sauvignon Blanc would match well, or enjoy a dry Vouvray.

Dungeness Crab *and* Yuba Rolls *with* Parsnips

Serves 4

2	medium parsnips	2
1	ripe avocado	1
1	lime, halved	1
8 oz	cooked and cleaned Dungeness crabmeat	225 g
½ tsp	pure vanilla extract	2.5 mL
2 Tbsp	yuzu mayonnaise (page 23)	30 mL
½	lemon	½
	Pinch of Maldon salt	
4 sheets	yuba	4 sheets
1 recipe	cooked and seasoned sushi rice (page 241)	1 recipe
1 Tbsp	prepared wasabi	15 mL
2 Tbsp	pickled ginger	30 mL
½ cup	citrus-soy dressing (page 237)	125 mL

Crab and parsnip go together very well, and Victor Pulleyblank, our Raw Bar chef, often pairs them. Yuba is a soybean sheet, also known as bean curd skin, that makes a nice change from nori. You can find it at Japanese food stores.

Rolling sushi gets easier as you practise. You will need a sushi mat lined with plastic wrap, a cutting board, a sharp knife and a damp towel. Be sure all of your ingredients and your equipment are ready before you start assembling the rolls. Also make sure the rice does not get too cold, or the grains will become too hard.

BRING A LARGE pot of water to a boil on medium heat. While the water is heating, cut the parsnips lengthwise into 3-inch/7.5-cm sections. Slice these pieces into ¼ inch/5 mm wide strips. Finally, cut these strips in half again to produce strips ⅛ inch/3 mm wide and 3 inches/7.5 cm long. You will need 32 of these strips.

Fill a large bowl with ice water. Immerse the parsnip strips in the boiling water and cook until soft through the centre, 3 to 4 minutes. Using a slotted spoon, transfer the strips to the bowl of ice water to stop the cooking process. Once they have cooled, dry them with a tea towel. Set aside.

Halve the avocado lengthwise, then remove and discard the pit. Cut each half in half again lengthwise, then slide a knife just under the skin of each segment and peel it off. Discard the avocado skins. Thinly slice the avocado along its length onto a plate, then squeeze lime juice over the slices so they retain their colour.

continued overleaf...

In a small bowl, combine the crabmeat and vanilla extract. Add the yuzu mayonnaise. Squeeze the lemon juice into the crabmeat, then season with salt. Mix until well combined.

Place one yuba sheet on top of the sushi mat. With wet hands, gather ½ cup/120 mL of rice. Lightly shape the rice into a football-like mound and place it in the middle of the yuba sheet. Using your fingers, spread the rice evenly across the sheet, leaving a 1-inch/2.5-cm gap at the top and bottom. If the rice starts sticking, wet your hands again.

Arrange 8 pieces of parsnip and ¼ of the avocado in a horizontal line across the middle of the rice and cover the line with ¼ of the crabmeat.

Holding the bottom edge of the sushi mat in your right hand, lift it to fold the bottom edge of the yuba sheet over the filling. Hold the top edge of the sushi mat with your left hand, and with your right hand pull the sushi mat back toward you, over the roll, to press the filling tightly. Lift the top edge of the sushi mat again and in one swift motion use your right hand to roll the sushi into a log. Once you reach the end of the yuba, make sure the seam side of the roll is down, then press firmly and remove the sushi mat. Rub your knife with a damp towel and cut the roll into 8 pieces. Repeat with the remaining filling and yuba sheets to make 4 rolls.

TO SERVE Arrange each roll on an individual plate. Position a small spoonful of wasabi and a quarter of the pickled ginger beside the sushi rolls. Serve with individual dipping bowls of the citrus-soy dressing.

WINE Premier cru Chablis is lovely with this roll, or pair it with a lightly oaked Sonoma Coast Chardonnay.

Red Tuna Rolls *with* Cucumber *and* Ponzu Sauce

Serves 4

The soft tuna and the crunchy cucumber in these rolls make for a nice contrast. However, it's the ponzu sauce served with these that I like so much I could drink it, though it's really the citrus tang of the yuzu juice in the sauce that I love. When I was the chef at the Canadian embassy in Rome, the ambassador and his wife ate sushi every Friday.

For tips on rolling sushi, see page 162.

CUT THE CUCUMBER into 3-inch/7.5-cm sections. Slice these pieces into strips ¼ inch/5 mm wide. Finally, cut these strips in half again to produce strips ⅛ inch/3 mm wide by 3 inches/7.5 cm long. You will need 24 of these strips. Cut the tuna into ½-inch/5-mm dice.

Place one piece of nori on top of the sushi mat. With wet hands, gather a small handful of rice. Lightly shape the rice into a football-like mound and place it in the middle of the nori sheet. Using your fingers, spread the rice evenly across the sheet, and extending it a ½ inch/1 cm over the top edge of the nori. If the rice starts sticking, wet your hands again. Sprinkle a quarter of the sesame seeds over the rice.

Carefully pick up and turn over the rice-covered nori sheet and place it, rice side down, on the sushi mat. Make sure that the overhanging bit of rice is at the top end of the mat. Spread a quarter of the yuzu mayonnaise horizontally across the middle of the nori. Arrange 6 strips of cucumber along the line of mayonnaise and top with a quarter of the tuna. Do not overfill the roll or it will be harder to seal.

continued overleaf...

1	English cucumber	1
8 oz	sashimi-grade yellowfin tuna loin	225 g
2	nori sheets, halved	2
1 recipe	cooked and seasoned sushi rice (page 241)	1 recipe
2 Tbsp	toasted black sesame seeds	30 mL
4 Tbsp	yuzu mayonnaise (page 23)	60 mL
1 Tbsp	prepared wasabi	15 mL
2 Tbsp	pickled ginger	30 mL
½ cup	ponzu sauce (page 237)	125 mL

Holding the bottom edge of the sushi mat in your right hand, lift it to fold the bottom edge of the nori sheet over the filling. Hold the top edge of the sushi mat with your left hand, and with your right hand pull the sushi mat back toward you, over the roll, to press the filling tightly. Lift the top edge of the sushi mat again and in one swift motion, use your right hand to roll the sushi into a log. Once you reach the end of the nori, make sure the seam side of the roll is down, then press firmly and remove the sushi mat. Rub your knife with a damp towel and cut the roll into 8 pieces. Repeat with the remaining filling and nori sheets to make 4 rolls.

TO SERVE Arrange each roll on an individual plate. Position a small spoonful of wasabi and a quarter of the pickled ginger beside the sushi rolls. Serve with individual dipping bowls of the citrus-soy dressing.

WINE Unoaked B.C. Pinot Gris would fun here, or try a fuller-bodied Alsatian white.

Sautéed Rainbow Trout *with* Fennel, Sundried Tomatoes *and* Capers

Serves 4

FENNEL SALAD

1 bulb	fennel	1 bulb
8	red radishes (such as French Breakfast radishes)	8
1 head	Belgian endive, leaves separated and rinsed	1 head
1 cup	sugar snap peas, blanched in salted water for 90 seconds and refreshed in ice water	240 mL
⅓ cup	olive oil	80 mL
3 cloves	garlic, halved	3 cloves
1	whole star anise	1
2 Tbsp	capers, rinsed	30 mL
3 Tbsp	sundried tomatoes in oil, cut in thin strips	45 mL
	Juice of 1 lemon	
1	lemon, cut in wedges	1

This dish can really be made at any time of year because fresh trout is always available. It goes well with fennel, which we use a lot at the restaurant as it has an unbeatable fresh quality, a crisp texture and a subtle, refreshing anise flavour. Choose a large bulb of fennel to make this salad.

FENNEL SALAD With a mandoline, a vegetable slicer or a sharp knife, slice the fennel widthwise as thinly as possible. Discard the bottom and any hard parts of the core. Thinly slice the radishes. Place the fennel and radish slices in a bowl of ice water with the endive leaves (if the endive leaves are large, cut them in half lengthwise) and allow to crisp for 10 minutes. Drain the vegetables and pat them dry. In a large dry bowl, combine the fennel, radishes, endive and snap peas. Set aside.

Heat the olive oil in a small saucepan on medium heat, add the garlic and star anise and sauté until the garlic is nicely browned, about 5 minutes. Remove from the heat, then remove and discard the garlic and star anise. Add the capers, sundried tomatoes and lemon juice to the warm oil. Set aside.

PANCETTA-WRAPPED TROUT Arrange the pancetta on a clean work surface. Place a trout fillet along the bottom edge of each pancetta slice. Sprinkle the trout evenly with rosemary and lightly season with salt and freshly ground pepper. Fold the bottom of the pancetta over the fish, then tightly roll the trout in the pancetta until you have four log-shaped packages. Wrap each package tightly in plastic wrap and refrigerate until chilled, about 30 minutes.

Remove the pancetta-wrapped fillets from the plastic wrap. In a sauté pan, heat the grapeseed oil on medium heat. Add the trout fillets, working in batches if necessary to avoid crowding the pan, and sauté for 3 to 4 minutes per side, until the pancetta is crisp. Drain on paper towels.

TO SERVE Toss the warm sundried tomato and caper oil with the fennel salad and mix gently to combine. Season with salt, if necessary. Divide the fennel among four plates and top with a fillet of trout. With a spoon, drizzle each plate with any leftover oil from the salad and serve with lemon wedges.

WINE Dry Rieslings, like those from Austria or Australia, stand up well to the tomatoes and the rest of the flavours, or have fun with different dry rosés, including some of the several good B.C. ones.

PANCETTA-WRAPPED TROUT

4 slices	pancetta, each 1 × 5 inches/ 2.5 × 12.5 cm	4 slices
4	trout fillets, each 5 to 6 oz/ 140 to 170 g, skin on but pin bones removed	4
1 tsp	chopped fresh rosemary	5 mL
1 Tbsp	grapeseed oil	15 mL

Miso-crusted Sablefish *with* Smoked Tuna Broth *and* Soba Noodles

Serves 4

SMOKED TUNA BROTH

4 cups	water	1 L
1-inch piece	fresh ginger, peeled and roughly chopped	2.5-cm piece
1 stalk	lemon grass, sliced	1 stalk
1 small piece	dried kombu seaweed	1 small piece
¼ cup packed	bonito flakes	60 mL packed
2 Tbsp	light soy sauce	30 mL
1 ½ Tbsp	rice vinegar	25 mL
¼ cup	thinly sliced shiitake mushrooms	60 mL
1 cup	soba noodles, cooked al dente and refreshed in cold water	240 mL
2	green onions, thinly sliced and placed in ice water	2

MISO-CRUSTED SABLEFISH

½ cup	miso paste	120 mL
2 Tbsp	sake	30 mL
1 ½ cups	granulated sugar	355 mL
4 fillets	sablefish, each 5 oz/140 g, skin on	4 fillets

When I opened our sister restaurant Blue Water Cafe, I put this dish on the menu there. It is based on a traditional Japanese preparation that works really well with moist white fish. The broth is also great as a soup or as a stock for cooking vegetables.

SMOKED TUNA BROTH Place the water in a medium saucepan, add the ginger, lemon grass and kombu and bring to a simmer on medium heat. Remove the saucepan from the heat, add the bonito flakes and allow the broth to stand uncovered for 10 minutes. Stir in the soy sauce and rice vinegar, then strain the broth through a fine-mesh sieve into a clean saucepan, discarding the solids. Set aside.

MISO-CRUSTED SABLEFISH Place the miso and sake into a large stainless bowl set over a pot of simmering water. Whisk until the sake is incorporated, then mix in the sugar. Turn off the heat and allow the mixture to stand over the hot water for 10 minutes to dissolve the sugar. Set aside and allow to cool for 30 minutes, then add the sablefish. Allow it to marinate for 30 minutes.

Preheat the oven to 400°F/205°C. Remove the sablefish from the marinade, scrape off and discard the excess miso and place the fish, skin side down, on a non-stick baking sheet. Bake for 8 minutes until the coating is lightly caramelized. Remove from the oven and allow the fillets to rest for 2 minutes.

TO SERVE Heat the broth on low heat. Add the mushrooms and soba noodles and warm until they are heated through, about 4 minutes. Divide the noodles and mushrooms

among 4 bowls, then top each serving with a fillet of sable-fish. Sprinkle with the green onions and serve immediately.

WINE I am partial to Riesling; sip top-quality Mosel Riesling or a B.C. one from Tantalus Vineyards or Wild Goose Winery.

Arctic Char *with* Salsify, Crosnes *and* Rutabaga *with* Lemon Butter

Serves 4

CONFIT OF VEGETABLES

1 cup	crosnes	240 mL
1 Tbsp	baking soda	15 mL
4 cups	duck fat	1 L
1	bay leaf	1
1	rutabaga, peeled and cut into ¼-inch/ 5-mm slices	1
4	salsify roots	4

Arctic char is a perfect substitute for salmon in many recipes; in this dish, we pan-fry the fish so the skin becomes nice and crisp. North Arm Farm in Pemberton provides the restaurant with many vegetables, including crosnes, which are also known as Chinese artichokes. Cooking these and the other vegetables in duck fat may seem a bit strange, but it enhances their flavour. Look for duck fat at fine grocery stores or at your local butcher shop.

CONFIT OF VEGETABLES Bring a medium pot of water to a boil on high heat and add a generous pinch of salt. Add the crosnes, followed immediately by the baking soda (it will foam a bit then subside) and cook for 6 minutes. Drain in a colander, then place the colander under cold running water and rub the crosnes around the colander to loosen the skins. Peel off and discard the skins, then transfer the crosnes to a large bowl and refrigerate until chilled, about 30 minutes.

Melt the duck fat in a medium saucepan on low heat, then add the bay leaf and the rutabaga. Peel the salsify roots and add them to the pot. Increase the heat until small bubbles begin to form in the fat, then reduce the heat to low, cover the vegetables with parchment paper and cook gently for 20 minutes. Using a slotted spoon, transfer the salsify to a small bowl and cook the rutabaga for a further 15 minutes. Transfer the rutabaga to the bowl of salsify. (The duck fat can be saved for 7 days in the fridge or frozen up to 1 month and used to confit other vegetables or duck.)

continued overleaf...

ARCTIC CHAR

4 fillets	Arctic char, each 5 oz/140 g, skin on but bones removed	4 fillets
2 cloves	garlic, thinly sliced	2 cloves
3 sprigs	fresh thyme, leaves only	3 sprigs
2 Tbsp	grapeseed oil	30 mL
1 Tbsp	unsalted butter	15 mL
⅛ cup	lemon butter (page 236), melted	30 mL

ARCTIC CHAR Arrange the fillets, flesh side down, on a cutting board. Using a sharp knife, make five or six incisions, each 1 inch/2.5 cm long, about a quarter of the way into the fish. Press a quarter of the garlic and a quarter of the thyme leaves into the incisions on each fillet.

Heat the grapeseed oil and the unsalted butter in a large saucepan on medium heat. Season the char with salt and pepper, then place the fish skin side down in the pan and cook for 5 to 6 minutes, or until the skin is golden brown and crispy. Remove the pan from the heat, turn the fillets over and allow the char to rest in the pan for 2 to 3 minutes. Transfer the fish to a plate and keep warm.

TO SERVE Place the rutabaga and salsify in a sauté pan on medium heat and allow them to caramelize in their own juices, about 5 minutes. Turn the vegetables over and add the crosnes. Heat for 3 minutes, or until the crosnes are warmed through. Divide the vegetables among 4 plates, top each serving with a fillet of Arctic char, then drizzle with the melted lemon butter. Serve immediately.

WINE Premier or grand cru Chablis has the acidity to match this dish, as does white Rioja or Rueda from Spain.

Nova Scotia Lobster *with* Bouillabaisse Sauce *and* Couscous

Serves 4

Sometimes when I'm experimenting with new recipes I put together several elements that might work, and sometimes they surprise me with just how well the flavours and textures complement one another. This recipe is one of those cases; in fact, unlike most of the other plates featured here, this is a dish I developed for the book that found its way onto the menu, not the other way around. You can also grill the lobsters lightly instead of broiling them.

LOBSTER Fill a large pot fitted with a lid with water and bring to a boil on high heat. Add about 1 Tbsp/15 mL of salt for every 4 cups/1 L of water. Plunge the lobsters into the water, cover and cook for 4 minutes. Using tongs, remove the lobsters from the pot, transfer them to a bowl and refrigerate until cool, about 30 minutes.

Once the lobsters are cool enough to handle, use a sharp knife to remove the claws. Using a nutcracker or a mallet, crack the claws and use a fork or a pick to remove the meat. Crack the knuckles and remove the meat. Place the lobsters on their backs and cut them in half lengthwise; the meat will be about half cooked. Clean out the lobster bodies, reserving the green tomalley (if you like it) but discarding all the innards, including the digestive tract down the tail. Rinse out the lobsters under cold running water. Arrange the claw and knuckle meat (save the tomalley for another use; it can be refrigerated in an airtight container for 1 day) inside the body cavities, place the lobsters on a baking sheet and spread them with the lemon butter.

continued overleaf...

LOBSTER

4	live lobsters, each 1¼ lbs/565 g, chilled in the freezer for 20 to 30 minutes to make them easier to handle	4
6 oz	lemon butter (page 236), softened	170 g

BOUILLABAISSE SAUCE

1 cup	olive oil	250 mL
3 oz	onions, sliced (about 1 small onion)	85 g
5 oz	sliced fennel (about 1 small bulb)	140 g
1 stalk	celery, sliced	1 stalk
1	carrot, sliced	1
½ cup	roughly chopped tomatoes	120 mL
1 clove	garlic, crushed	1 clove
1 sprig	fresh thyme	1 sprig
1	bay leaf	1
3 cups	fish stock (page 233)	750 mL
½ tsp	saffron	2.5 mL

BOUILLABAISSE SAUCE In a medium saucepan fitted with a lid, heat ½ cup/125 mL of the olive oil on medium heat. Add the onions, fennel, celery, carrots, tomatoes, garlic, thyme and bay leaf and sauté for 5 minutes or until the vegetables are soft. Reduce the heat to low, cover and simmer for 10 minutes to allow the flavours to develop.

Add the fish stock and the saffron and simmer for another 15 minutes. Remove from the heat, allow to cool slightly and then transfer to a blender or a food processor and purée until smooth. Press the sauce through a fine-mesh sieve, discarding the solids, and whisk in the remaining olive oil. Set aside. Will keep refrigerated in an airtight container for up to 3 days.

COUSCOUS Place the chicken (or vegetable) stock in a small pot and bring it to a boil on medium heat. Turn off the heat.

Place the couscous in a medium bowl, pour the hot stock over it and stir until well mixed. Cover the bowl with plastic wrap and allow the couscous to stand for 25 to 30 minutes, fluffing it with a fork or a whisk every 10 minutes. Stir in the pistachios, apricots, currants, lemon juice and lemon zest.

FINISH LOBSTERS Preheat the oven to 425°F/220°C. Cook the lobsters for 5 to 6 minutes, allowing the butter to melt and the meat to cook completely.

TO SERVE Gently heat the bouillabaisse sauce in a small saucepan on low heat; be careful not to boil it. Spoon a ¼ cup/60 mL of the sauce onto the centre of each plate. Stir the mint, cilantro and vinaigrette into the couscous, then mound a quarter of it over each serving of sauce. Top the couscous with a lobster, then drizzle any butter from the pan over the lobsters.

WINE The finest white Burgundy is perfect here, or buy local with an outstanding B.C. Chardonnay, such as Cedar Creek Estate Winery's Platinum Reserve.

COUSCOUS

1¼ cups	chicken or vegetable stock (pages 235, 233)	315 mL
1½ cups	fine couscous	355 mL
½ cup	pistachios, shelled and toasted	120 mL
¼ cup	dried apricots, soaked in water, then drained and chopped	60 mL
¼ cup	currants, soaked in water, then drained	60 mL
	Juice and zest of 1 lemon	
1 Tbsp	chopped fresh mint	15 mL
1 Tbsp	chopped fresh cilantro	15 mL
3 Tbsp	basic vinaigrette (page 236)	45 mL

Scallops *with* Corn, Spicy Sausage *and* Mustard Vinaigrette

Serves 4

MUSTARD VINAIGRETTE

⅓ cup	extra-virgin olive oil	80 mL
¼ cup	grainy mustard	60 mL
⅓ cup	maple vinegar	80 mL
2 Tbsp	honey	30 mL

CORN

2 cups	vegetable stock (page 233)	500 mL
½ cup	whipping cream	125 mL
4 cobs	fresh corn, shucked	4 cobs
1 Tbsp	grapeseed oil	15 mL
2	shallots, minced	2
1 oz	minced bacon (about 2 to 3 slices)	30 g
¼ tsp	red chili flakes	1 mL

SCALLOPS

2 Tbsp	grapeseed oil	30 mL
2	chorizo sausages, each cut in 6 diagonal slices	2
16	large fresh Pacific scallops	16
⅓ cup	baby herbs or lettuces, for garnish	80 mL

This recipe uses our own version of creamed corn. As we do in this recipe, be sure to reserve raw corn cobs to make soup stocks: much of corn's flavour is held in the cob. At Araxi, we make a homemade chorizo sausage for this dish, so choose a spicy sausage. Maple vinegar is readily available in fine grocery stores.

MUSTARD VINAIGRETTE Combine all of the ingredients in a small bowl and whisk to blend. Will keep refrigerated in an airtight container for up to 3 days.

CORN Place the vegetable stock and the cream in a medium saucepan. Cut the kernels off the corn cobs, then chop the cobs into 2-inch/5-cm pieces. Reserve the kernels in a small bowl and add the cobs to the stock-cream mixture. Bring to a boil on medium heat, then reduce the heat to low and simmer for 10 minutes.

In a separate saucepan, heat the grapeseed oil on medium heat. Add the shallots and bacon and sauté until softened and lightly golden, about 4 minutes. Add the chili flakes and cook for 1 minute. Stir in the corn kernels and mix them well with the bacon and shallots.

Strain the corn stock through a fine-mesh sieve into the corn kernel mixture. Discard the cobs. Reduce the heat to medium and cook until the liquid is almost evaporated and the corn is a creamy texture, about 10 minutes. Cover the pot, remove from the heat and set aside.

SCALLOPS Heat the grapeseed oil on medium-high heat in a medium sauté pan. Add the chorizo and sauté until crisp and browned, about 2 minutes per side. Using tongs, transfer the sausages to a plate and keep warm. Pour off some of the oil.

Season the scallops with salt and add them to the pan. Sauté on one side for 2 minutes, then remove the pan from the heat and allow it to stand for 1 minute. Turn the scallops over and quickly remove them from the pan.

TO SERVE Heap a quarter of the creamed corn in the centre of each plate. Alternate the scallops and pieces of chorizo around the corn. Drizzle the mustard vinaigrette on and around the scallops, top with baby herbs (or lettuces) and serve immediately.

WINE A full-flavoured white like Austrian Grüner Veltliner or Russian River Chardonnay will hold up to this dish, or try a medium red Burgundy, such as Volnay.

Fresh Noodles *with* Manila Clams, Swiss Chard *and* Kale

Serves 4 to 6

1 recipe	fresh pasta dough (page 241)	1 recipe
4 Tbsp	olive oil	60 mL
2	shallots, thinly sliced	2
1	small bird's eye or jalapeño pepper, minced	1
1½ lbs	Manila clams	680 g
¼ cup	dry white wine	60 mL
2 cups	mixed kale and Swiss chard, stems removed and leaves roughly chopped	480 mL
2 Tbsp	unsalted butter	30 mL
¼ cup	grated Parmesan cheese (optional)	60 mL

I have listed the cheese as optional in this recipe because, in Italy, cheese is not always served on seafood-based pastas. Note that if you do not have a pasta cutter, you can fold the pasta like a jellyroll and use a knife to cut the sheets into strips of fettuccine. The Swiss chard and kale really make this dish—their earthy flavours are fantastic—but be sure to use only firm leaves. Add more chilies, if you like spicy foods.

DIVIDE THE PASTA dough into 3 equal portions. Following the instructions on your pasta machine, roll each portion of dough into a sheet with the thickness of a quarter. Use your machine's cutter attachment to cut the pasta sheets into fettuccine.

Place a wooden broomstick across two counter tops or set up a pasta drying rack. Hang the fettuccine over the broomstick (or on the drying rack) and allow to dry for at least 30 minutes.

Fill a large pot with water and bring it to a boil on high heat. Add about 1 tsp/5 mL of salt for every 4 cups/1 L of water.

In a large shallow pan fitted with a lid, heat 2 Tbsp/ 30 mL of the olive oil on medium heat. Add the shallots and the bird's eye (or jalapeño) peppers and cook for 2 to 3 minutes to soften them. Increase the heat to high, then add the clams and the white wine. Cover and allow the clams to steam for 2 minutes. Add the kale and Swiss chard, cover and cook for another 2 minutes.

Drop the fettuccine into the pot of boiling water, stir it once and cook for exactly 2 minutes, no longer. Drain the pasta, then add it to the clam mixture. Once all the clams have opened, add the remaining olive oil and the butter. (Discard any clams that do not open.) Toss gently to combine.

TO SERVE Divide the pasta among individual bowls, being sure to evenly share the clams and the greens. Sprinkle with the Parmesan cheese, if desired.

WINE Experiment with regional, indigenous Italian whites such as Greco di Tufo, Fiano di Avellino, Falanghina or Sicilian blends.

Saddle *of* Rabbit *with* Buttered Noodles, Carrots *and* Mustard Sauce

Serves 4

BUTTERED NOODLES

½ recipe	fresh pasta dough (page 241)	½ recipe
	OR	
9 oz	fresh store-bought pasta (preferably fettuccine)	250 g
½ cup	vegetable nage (page 233)	125 mL
3 Tbsp	unsalted butter	45 mL

SADDLE OF RABBIT

2	whole saddles of rabbit, each 10 to 12 oz/285 to 340 g, bones removed	2
8	baby carrots, blanched or honey-coated	8
2 sprigs	fresh lemon thyme, leaves only	2 sprigs
12 thin slices	pancetta or bacon	12 thin slices
2 Tbsp	grapeseed oil	30 mL
1 cup	mustard sauce (page 237)	250 mL

Sous-vide is the method I use to cook a lot of meats at Araxi and it involves vacuum-sealing food in a bag, then cooking it gently in a water bath at low temperature. For example, I usually cook the rabbit for this dish for 48 minutes at 136°F/58°C for the perfect result. Here, we've adapted the recipe to suit conventional ovens. The saddle is the part of the rabbit that runs between its fore and hind legs. The carrots are as natural a pairing for rabbit as the phrase "What's up, Doc?"

BUTTERED NOODLES To make the fresh pasta, divide the pasta dough into 3 equal portions. Following the instructions on your pasta machine, roll each portion of dough into a sheet with the thickness of a quarter. Use your machine's cutter attachment to cut the pasta sheets into fettuccine. Set aside.

SADDLE OF RABBIT Preheat the oven to 350°C/175°C. Place the two rabbit pieces on a clean work surface. Trim and discard any excess fat, then use a sharp knife to scrape the belly flaps and trim them so they are even. Gently score the flaps in a cross-hatch pattern. You will notice that the loins are quite wide at one end and thinner at the other. On each saddle, pull off the small tenderloin piece that is at the wide end and place it beside the thin end of the loin. (This will even out the cooking time.)

Arrange 4 carrots between the two loins of each saddle and season them with salt and pepper and lemon thyme leaves. Roll up the rabbit as you would a sushi roll and cut each roll in half widthwise to obtain four portions.

continued overleaf…

CARROT PURÉE

3 ½ lbs	carrots, peeled	1.6 kg
½ tsp	mild curry powder	5 mL
1 Tbsp	unsalted butter	15 mL

On a clean work surface, arrange 3 strips of pancetta (or bacon) with a short edge toward you and the long sides just touching each other. Place a rabbit roll across the pancetta strips, at the end closest to you. Tightly roll the pancetta around the rabbit. Repeat with the remaining pancetta and rabbit rolls.

Cut 4 pieces of plastic wrap, each 5 × 8 inches/12.5 × 20 cm. Set the sheets of plastic wrap on the work surface and place a rabbit roll in the middle of each one. Fold the bottom half of the plastic wrap over the roll, then tightly roll the rabbit in the plastic wrap, forming a nice log shape. Cut 4 pieces of aluminum foil and wrap each of the plastic-wrapped rabbit rolls in a sheet of foil. Place the foil packages in the oven and cook for 18 to 20 minutes. Remove the rabbit from the oven and test for doneness using a meat thermometer (the internal temperature should be 155°F/68°C). Allow the rolls to rest, unwrapped, for 5 minutes until serving.

CARROT PURÉE Cut the carrots in half widthwise. Separate the thicker top parts from the thinner bottom pieces. Cut the top parts into chunks, place them in a juicer and juice them for about 2 cups/500 mL of juice. (If you do not have a juicer, cook half the carrots in water until tender.) Slice the bottom parts into thin rounds and place them in a small saucepan. Cover the carrots with the carrot juice (or cooked carrots) and add the curry powder. Cook on medium heat until the carrots are very soft, about 10 minutes. Drain the juice into a small bowl and transfer the carrots to a food processor or a blender. Purée the carrots, adding enough of the juice to obtain a smooth consistency. Mix in the butter, season lightly with salt and set aside.

FINISH RABBIT Unwrap the rabbit, discarding the foil and plastic wrap. Heat the grapeseed oil in a large sauté pan on medium-high heat, add the rabbit and sear for 2 minutes to crisp the pancetta. Transfer the rabbit to a plate, pour off any excess oil in the pan and add the mustard sauce. Reduce the heat to low and cook the sauce until it is warmed through.

FINISH NOODLES Heat the vegetable nage in a medium saucepan on medium heat.

Fill a large pot with water and bring it to a boil on high heat. Add about 1 tsp/5 mL of salt for every 4 cups/1 L of water. Drop the fettuccine into the water, stir it once and cook for 2 minutes. (If you are using store-bought pasta, cook it until it is al dente, or according to package directions.) Drain the pasta, then add it to the nage. Stir in the butter and lightly season the noodles with salt.

TO SERVE Slice each rabbit roll into 3 pieces. Spin a quarter of the noodles on a carving fork and place them on a plate. Repeat with the remaining 3 plates. Spoon a quarter of the carrot purée beside the noodles. Top each plate with 3 slices of rabbit and spoonfuls of the mustard sauce.

WINE I love to pair rabbit with Italian reds, from Barolo and Barbaresco to Chianti Classico and Brunello.

Crispy Duck Confit *with* Lentils *and* Honey-roasted Carrots

Serves 4

DUCK CONFIT

4	large duck legs, tip of the drumsticks cut off	4
2 cloves	garlic, sliced	2 cloves
4 tsp	kosher salt	20 mL
2 sprigs	fresh thyme, leaves only	2 sprigs
2	bay leaves, crushed	2
2¼ lbs	duck fat	1 kg

You can make duck confit in large batches since it keeps very well. And as an alternative to the warm lentils in this dish, you can serve lentils cold as a salad; they really soak up flavour. I like to cook carrots such as these honey-roasted ones in very little liquid so they cook in their own juices rather than losing all their goodness in a pot of boiling water. Look for duck fat at fine grocery stores or at your local butcher shop.

DUCK CONFIT Place a sheet of parchment paper on a baking sheet, then arrange the duck legs, skin side down, on the parchment paper. Divide the garlic evenly over the legs.

In a small bowl, combine the salt, thyme and bay leaves. Sprinkle this spice mixture liberally over the duck. Cover the duck with a second sheet of parchment paper, place another baking sheet on top and weight the baking sheet with a large can of vegetables. Refrigerate the duck legs for at least 12 to 24 hours.

Preheat the oven to 300°F/150°C. Melt the duck fat in a small saucepan on low heat. Remove the duck from the fridge, lift off the weights, the baking sheet and the parchment paper and rinse the meat under cold water to remove the salt and the herbs. Pat dry with a tea towel and place the duck legs in an ovenproof casserole fitted with a lid. Pour the melted fat over the duck, place the casserole dish on low heat and cook until the fat begins to bubble gently. Cover the duck with a clean sheet of parchment paper and cover the casserole with a lid. Bake in the oven for 1 hour and 45 minutes. To check that the duck is done, gently remove a leg from the casserole and place it on a plate. Grip the drumstick bone and turn it; if it moves easily, the bird is cooked. Remove the casserole from the oven and allow the meat to cool in the fat. Will keep refrigerated in an airtight container for up to 2 weeks.

LENTILS Heat the butter in a medium saucepan on low heat. Add the carrots, celery, onions and thyme and sauté for 5 minutes to soften. Rinse the lentils in a colander under cold water, then add them to the pot. Increase the heat to medium and add the vegetable stock. Bring the mixture to a boil then reduce the heat to low and simmer for 20 minutes. The liquid will reduce while the lentils cook, so add a little more stock or water if the lentils begin to stick. The lentils are cooked when they are tender but hold their shape. Remove the pot from the heat, drain off any excess liquid, remove the thyme sprigs and, while the lentils are still warm, stir in the vinaigrette.

HONEY-ROASTED CARROTS Heat the olive oil in a shallow saucepan on medium heat. Add the carrots, season with salt and sauté for 2 to 3 minutes. Add the honey, pepper-corns and bay leaf and toss with the carrots. Reduce the heat to medium-low.

Add the vegetable stock and cook until the stock has evaporated and the carrots are tender and coated with the honey and their juices, about 8 minutes. Discard the bay leaf. Set the carrots aside and keep warm.

continued overleaf…

LENTILS

2 Tbsp	unsalted butter	30 mL
1	carrot, peeled and cut in ¼-inch/ 5-mm dice	1
2 stalks	celery, cut in ¼-inch/5-mm dice	2 stalks
1	small onion, minced	1
2 sprigs	fresh thyme	2 sprigs
¾ cup	small Puy lentils	180 mL
3 cups	vegetable stock (page 233)	750 mL
3 Tbsp	basic vinaigrette (page 236)	45 mL
2 Tbsp	fresh chopped parsley	30 mL

HONEY-ROASTED CARROTS

2 Tbsp	olive oil	30 mL
12 to 14	plump baby carrots, peeled	12 to 14
2 Tbsp	honey	30 mL
5	white peppercorns, crushed	5
1	bay leaf	1
¾ cup	vegetable stock (page 233)	185 mL

FINISH DUCK CONFIT Preheat the oven to 350°F/175°C. Remove the duck legs from the fat and place them, skin side down, in an ovenproof sauté pan on medium-high heat. Once the skin starts to crisp, 5 to 6 minutes, place the pan in the oven for 8 to 10 minutes, until the duck is heated through.

TO SERVE Stir the parsley into the lentils and season with salt and pepper. Divide the lentils among 4 bowls, top each serving with a duck leg and garnish with the carrots.

WINE This dish is magic with bold Oregon Pinot Noir or hearty red Burgundy such as Vosne-Romanée or Morey-St-Denis.

Braised Beef Short Ribs *with* Cauliflower Purée *and* Pickled Mushrooms

Serves 4

If you can find them, use Kobe-style beef short ribs; in other words, the more marbling in the meat, the better, because more fat means moister cooked ribs. The pickled mushrooms in this recipe have a great texture and keep well, if you have leftovers.

PICKLED MUSHROOMS Heat the pickling brine in a medium saucepan on medium heat and add the shallots, thyme and bay leaf. Once the brine is simmering, stir in the wild and cultivated mushrooms and turn off the heat. Allow the mushrooms to cool and soften in the liquid. Will keep refrigerated in an airtight container for up to 3 days.

SHORT RIBS Preheat the oven to 300°F/150°C.

On the cheesecloth, place the parsley, thyme and bay leaf. Gather the edges of the cheesecloth and tie them together tightly with kitchen twine to make a bouquet garni.

Place the red wine in a medium saucepan, bring to a boil on high heat and immediately reduce the heat to medium. Simmer the wine until it is reduced by half, about 10 minutes.

Heat the grapeseed oil in an ovenproof casserole fitted with a lid on high heat. Season the short ribs with salt and pepper, then add them to the pan. Sauté uncovered until deep brown on all sides, about 4 minutes, then transfer the short ribs to a cooling rack. Reduce the heat to medium.

Drain excess oil from the pan, then stir in the garlic, shallots, carrots and celery and gently sauté them until lightly golden, about 8 minutes. Add the short ribs, the red wine reduction and the veal stock. Bring to a boil on medium heat, then add the bouquet garni, cover and place in the oven for 3½ hours or until the meat is very tender.

continued overleaf...

PICKLED MUSHROOMS

2 cups	sweet pickling brine (page 232)	500 mL
2	shallots, thinly sliced	2
2 sprigs	fresh thyme	2 sprigs
1	bay leaf	1
2 cups	torn pieces of fresh wild mushrooms (such as chanterelle, cauliflower, pine, black trumpet)	480 mL
1 cup	torn pieces of cultivated mushrooms (such as cremini, maitake, oyster)	240 mL

Remove the short ribs from the braising liquid and allow them to cool. Strain the liquid through a fine-mesh sieve or a cheesecloth into a small saucepan, discarding the solids. Cook on medium heat to reduce the liquid to a saucelike consistency, about 20 minutes. Trim the cooled ribs of any excess fat, place them in the reduced sauce and warm them through, about 10 minutes.

CAULIFLOWER PURÉE Heat the butter in a medium saucepan on medium heat. Add the onions and sauté until softened but not coloured, about 8 minutes. Add the cauliflower, lightly season with salt and cook for 2 to 3 minutes to release the flavours. Be careful not to brown the vegetables. Add the cream, reduce the heat to low and simmer for 10 to 12 minutes, until the cauliflower is very tender and the cream has reduced.

Drain any remaining cream into a small bowl. Purée the cauliflower in a blender or using a hand-held blender. Add enough cream to give the purée a smooth consistency. Press the purée through a fine-mesh sieve and season with salt and pepper. Reheat in a small pot on low heat.

TO SERVE In a small pot, reheat the mushrooms in a little of the pickling juices on low heat. Divide the cauliflower purée among 4 plates, arranging it in a pool in the centre. Top each serving with a short rib and some of its juices, and garnish with pickled mushrooms and a sprig of thyme.

WINE Pair these ribs with some big New World reds like Napa Cabernet Sauvignon, Barossa Shiraz, Argentine Malbec or even a powerful Italian red like Amarone. If you can, use some of your drinking wine in the recipe for best flavour.

SHORT RIBS

3-inch square	cheesecloth	7.5-cm square
2 sprigs	fresh parsley	2 sprigs
2 sprigs	fresh thyme	2 sprigs
1	bay leaf	1
4 cups	red wine	1 L
3 Tbsp	grapeseed oil	45 mL
4	beef short ribs, each 12 to 14 oz/340 to 400 g and containing 3 bones	4
3 cloves	garlic	3 cloves
5	shallots, quartered	5
1	medium carrot, peeled and roughly chopped	1
1 stalk	celery, roughly chopped	1 stalk
12 cups	veal stock (page 234)	3 L
4 sprigs	fresh thyme, for garnish	4 sprigs

CAULIFLOWER PURÉE

2 Tbsp	unsalted butter	30 mL
1	small onion, sliced	1
3 cups	cauliflower, in florets or small pieces	720 mL
2 cups	whipping cream	500 mL

Pepper-crusted Rib-eye Steaks *with* Wild Mushroom Ragout *and* Roasted Baby Beets

Serves 4

RIB-EYE STEAKS

1 Tbsp	black peppercorns	15 mL
1 tsp	white peppercorns	5 mL
2	rib-eye steaks, each 14 oz/400 g, bone in	2
2 Tbsp	Dijon mustard	30 mL
3 Tbsp	grapeseed oil	45 mL
2 Tbsp	unsalted butter	30 mL
1 cup	red wine sauce (page 239)	250 mL

ROASTED BEETS

1 lb	beets, skins on	455 g
1 sprig	fresh thyme	1 sprig
3 Tbsp	olive oil	45 mL

Try to find thick, well-marbled steaks for this recipe and be sure to let the cooked meats rest before serving them so they stay juicy. Don't be in a rush. The sweetness of the beets calms the strong pepper flavour of the steaks.

RIB-EYE STEAKS Combine the peppercorns on a clean work surface and use a heavy pan to crush them coarsely. With a spoon or a pastry brush, coat the steaks with the Dijon mustard, then sprinkle them with the peppercorns and season them with salt. Allow them to marinate for 15 minutes.

ROASTED BEETS Preheat the oven to 350°F/175°C. Cut 2 squares of aluminum foil, each 11 × 18 inches/30 × 45 cm, and place them one on top of the other on a clean work surface. Mound the beets in the centre of the foil and season them with salt and pepper. Add the thyme and pour the olive oil over them.

Fold the bottom edges of the foil over the beets, then fold the top edges over the bottom to completely encase the beets. Tuck in the sides of the foil like an envelope to seal the package. Transfer to a baking sheet and bake for 35 to 45 minutes until the beets are very soft when a knife is inserted into them. Remove them from the oven, unwrap the foil and allow them to cool slightly. Once the beets are cool enough to handle, rub them between your fingers to peel off the skins. Discard the foil and the skins. Quarter the beets and set aside.

continued overleaf...

WILD MUSHROOM RAGOUT

¼ cup	unsalted butter	60 mL
2	shallots, finely sliced	2
1⅛ lbs	wild mushrooms (such as chanterelles, porcini, pine), sliced	500 g
1 clove	garlic, minced	1 clove
1 Tbsp	lemon juice	15 mL
2 Tbsp	chopped fresh parsley	30 mL

WILD MUSHROOM RAGOUT In a medium sauté pan, heat the butter on medium heat. Add the shallots and sauté until they are soft, about 5 minutes. Stir in the mushrooms and garlic, season with salt and pepper, then cook for 8 to 10 minutes, until evenly browned. Remove the pan from the heat, add the lemon juice and parsley and set aside.

FINISH RIB-EYE STEAKS Preheat the oven to 400°F/205°C. In an ovenproof sauté pan, heat the grapeseed oil on high heat. Add the steaks and sear for 1 minute per side until they are deep brown and the pepper is toasted. Place the pan in the oven and cook for 4 minutes. Turn the steaks over. Add the butter to the pan and cook for another 3 minutes. Remove the pan from the oven and baste the steaks with their juices for 1 minute, then transfer the steaks to a plate and allow them to rest for at least 5 minutes. (The steaks should be medium rare; if you like them cooked more or if they are quite thick, cook them a little longer.)

While the steaks are resting, drain any excess fat from the pan, then add the red wine sauce and bring to a simmer. Cut the bones from the meat and slice each steak into 10 thin slices.

TO SERVE Fan 5 slices of steak on each plate and top each serving with a quarter of the red wine sauce. Spoon a quarter of the mushroom ragout over the steak and arrange the roasted beets around the plate.

WINE Enjoy some good Bordeaux, modern Rioja or Priorat reds, or serve a top Malbec from Argentina, which is a natural with beef.

Veal Sweetbreads *with* Pomme Purée, Brussels Sprouts *and* Persillade

Serves 4

A cook's dish is what I like to call this. In other words, most of the chefs who visit the restaurant order this from the menu. This recipe combines on one plate two foods—sweetbreads and Brussels sprouts—that I love but many people wrinkle their noses at. For variety, serve sunchoke purée (page 125) in place of the potatoes. Try it, you'll like it!

VEAL SWEETBREADS Soak the sweetbreads in a bowl of ice-cold water for 5 minutes. Pour off the water and repeat 4 times. Then place the sweetbreads in a medium bowl and cover with the milk. Cover the bowl and refrigerate the sweetbreads for 12 hours.

Place 2 Tbsp/30 mL of the butter in a medium saucepan on medium heat. Add the carrots, onions, celery and parsley and sauté for 6 minutes, or until the vegetables are softened.

Drain the milk from the sweetbreads and discard, rinse the veal and add it to the pot of vegetables along with the white wine, vegetable (or chicken) stock and bay leaf. Bring the mixture to a boil, then reduce the heat to low and simmer for 10 minutes. Remove from the heat and allow the sweetbreads to cool in the cooking liquid.

When the sweetbreads are cool enough to handle, remove them from the pot and peel off and discard the membranes and sinew. Place the cleaned sweetbreads on a tea towel and refrigerate them for 30 minutes, until chilled.

POMME PURÉE Place the potatoes in a large saucepan. Cover them with cold water and add a large pinch of salt.

continued overleaf...

VEAL SWEETBREADS

1 ½ lbs	very fresh veal sweetbreads	680 g
8 cups	whole milk	2 L
4 Tbsp	clarified butter (page 232)	60 mL
1	carrot, roughly chopped	1
1	onion, sliced	1
2 stalks	celery, chopped	2 stalks
2 sprigs	fresh parsley	2 sprigs
½ cup	white wine	125 mL
4 cups	vegetable or chicken stock (pages 233, 235)	1 L
1	bay leaf	1

POMME PURÉE

1½ lbs	medium potatoes (such as Désirée, Sieglinde or Yukon Gold), peeled, rinsed and cut into quarters	680 g
½ cup	whipping cream	125 mL
3 Tbsp	whole milk	45 mL
3 Tbsp	unsalted butter	45 mL
1 sprig	fresh thyme	1 sprig
1 clove	garlic, sliced in half	1 clove
1 tsp	kosher salt	5 mL

BRUSSELS SPROUTS

12 to 14	Brussels sprouts	12 to 14
2 oz	bacon (about 2 to 3 slices)	60 g
3	whole shallots	3
2 Tbsp	unsalted butter	30 mL

Bring the potatoes to a boil on high heat, then reduce the heat to medium and cook until they are quite tender when pierced with a fork, about 15 minutes. Reduce the heat to low.

Drain the potatoes in a colander, then return them to the pot and cook them for 5 to 6 minutes to remove any excess moisture.

In a smaller pot, heat the cream, milk, butter, thyme and garlic on medium heat until the mixture comes to a simmer. Remove from the heat and set aside.

While the potatoes are still warm, pass them through a food mill or a potato ricer into a large bowl. Strain the cream mixture over the potatoes, discarding the solids, and add the salt. Using a spatula, gently fold together the ingredients. Set aside and keep warm.

BRUSSELS SPROUTS Peel the outer leaves from the Brussels sprouts, then slice off the bottoms and cut the sprouts in half lengthwise. Discard the trimmings. Place the Brussels sprouts in a medium saucepan, add the bacon and the shallots and just enough water to cover. Bring the sprouts to a boil on high heat, then reduce the heat to medium and simmer for 8 to 10 minutes, or until the centres are soft. Drain the sprouts in a colander and transfer them to a sauté pan. Add the butter, season with salt and pepper and sauté on medium heat until lightly coloured, about 5 minutes. Remove from the heat and discard the bacon and shallots.

PERSILLADE Combine the shallots, garlic and parsley in a small bowl and set aside.

FINISH SWEETBREADS Heat the remaining 2 Tbsp/30 mL of the clarified butter in a large sauté pan on medium-high heat. Season the sweetbreads with salt and pepper, add them to the pan and cook them on one side for 2 to 3 minutes, or until golden brown. Turn them over and cook for another 3 to 4 minutes, until brown and heated through. Transfer the sweetbreads to paper towels to drain.

FINISH PERSILLADE Pour off any excess oil from the sweetbreads pan and return it to the heat. Add the butter, and when it starts to foam, stir in the parsley mixture. Sauté for 20 seconds, then mix in the lemon juice and the vegetable stock (or water). Remove from the heat.

TO SERVE Arrange 3 Tbsp/45 mL of pomme purée in a line down the middle of 4 individual plates and top with a quarter of the Brussels sprouts. Place the sweetbreads on the sprouts and spoon some of the persillade over the plate.

WINE Celebrate this dish with rosé Champagne, dry Spanish rosé or good-quality Pouilly-Fuissé.

PERSILLADE

1	shallot, minced	1
2 cloves	garlic, minced	2 cloves
¼ cup	chopped fresh curly-leaf parsley	60 mL
2 Tbsp	unsalted butter	30 mL
	Juice of 1 lemon	
3 Tbsp	vegetable stock (page 234) or water	45 mL

Roasted Rack of Lamb with Spaetzle and Parsley Roots

Serves 4

Great-quality lamb is becoming more available in British Columbia and Alberta, especially from the Peace River district, where the animals are larger and have a mild flavour. For this recipe, you will need a perforated pan or a spaetzle cutter to make the little dumplings known as spaetzle. This recipe makes a lot, so to store leftover spaetzle, allow the blanched dumplings to cool, then cover them lightly with oil and refrigerate them in an airtight container for up to 3 days. Parsley roots resemble small parsnips, taste like a cross between carrots and parsley, and have a wonderful soft texture. When deep-fried they make nice chips.

ROASTED LAMB Preheat the oven to 375°F/190°C. In a cast-iron pan or an ovenproof sauté pan, heat the olive oil on medium-high heat. Season the lamb liberally with salt and pepper, then place it in the pan, meat side down, and sear for 3 to 4 minutes until browned. Turn the lamb over and brown it for 3 to 4 minutes more. Lift the lamb off the pan, add the rosemary to the pan and set the lamb back down on the rosemary. Place the pan in the oven and roast for 10 minutes. Turn the lamb over and roast for 7 to 8 minutes longer. Remove from the oven and place the lamb in a warm place to rest for at least 10 minutes.

SPAETZLE Fill a large pot with salted water, making sure the water reaches to at least 3 to 4 inches/7.5 to 10 cm below the rim of the pot. Bring the water to a boil on high heat, then simmer on medium heat.

continued overleaf...

ROASTED LAMB

3 Tbsp	olive oil	45 mL
4	4-bone racks of lamb, each 8 to 9 oz/225 to 255 g	4
2 sprigs	fresh rosemary	2 sprigs
½ cup	salsa verde (page 58)	125 mL

SPAETZLE

2 ¼ cups	all-purpose flour	535 mL
1 tsp	salt	5 mL
6	eggs	6
¼ cup	whole milk	60 mL
2 Tbsp	grapeseed oil	30 mL
½ cup	vegetable nage or chicken stock (pages 233, 235)	125 mL
2 Tbsp	unsalted butter	30 mL
3 Tbsp	grated Parmesan cheese	45 mL

HONEY-GLAZED PARSLEY ROOTS

10 to 12	parsley roots, peeled and halved	10 to 12
2 Tbsp	grapeseed oil	30 mL
1 Tbsp	honey	15 mL

Place the flour in large mixing bowl and make a well in the centre. Add the salt, eggs and milk. Use a whisk to combine all the ingredients, switching to a wooden spoon as the mixture thickens. Beat the batter hard with the spoon, trying to incorporate as much air as possible, as this will enable the spaetzle to puff up when it is reheated. Once small bubbles form in the batter, after about 5 minutes, it is ready.

Fill a large bowl with ice water. Place a perforated pan or a spaetzle cutter over the pot of simmering water and, using a spatula or a palette knife, press the mixture through the pan (or cutter) in small batches. The dough will drop into the water, which cooks and forms the spaetzle. Once the spaetzle float to the surface of the pot, use a slotted spoon to transfer them to the ice water to stop the cooking. Once they have cooled completely, drain the spaetzle and set aside.

HONEY-GLAZED PARSLEY ROOTS Bring a medium pot of water to a boil on high heat. Add a pinch of salt and the parsley roots and cook for 4 minutes to soften. Drain the parsley roots and place them on a tea towel to dry.

While the parsley roots are still warm, place them in a sauté pan with the grapeseed oil and heat on medium heat until browned on all sides, about 3 minutes. Add the honey and cook for 2 minutes to further brown them. Set aside.

FINISH SPAETZLE In a sauté pan, heat the grapeseed oil on medium heat. Add 2 cups/480 mL of the spaetzle and cook for 2 to 3 minutes, or until they puff up and are golden brown. Add the vegetable nage (or chicken stock) and sauté until hot, about 3 minutes. Mix in the butter and Parmesan cheese and season lightly with salt and pepper.

TO SERVE Divide the spaetzle among 4 individual plates. Slice the lamb racks between the bones and place 4 pieces over the spaetzle on each plate. Arrange 2 to 3 pieces of parsley root on the lamb and drizzle the meat with salsa verde.

WINE Enjoy a variety of full reds here: worth seeking are wines from Madiran or Hermitage, France; Toro or Priorat, Spain; Washington Syrah and Meritage blends, or our own B.C. Syrah, such as the one from Road 13 Vineyards.

Roasted Portobello Mushrooms *with* Chickpea Fritters *and* Cucumber Yogurt

Serves 4

CHICKPEA FRITTERS

2 cups	cooked chickpeas	480 mL
¼ cup	all-purpose flour	60 mL
½ tsp	baking soda	2.5 mL
1 clove	garlic, chopped	1 clove
2 Tbsp	chopped onion	30 mL
1 Tbsp	roughly chopped fresh parsley	15 mL
1 Tbsp	roughly chopped fresh cilantro	15 mL
1	egg	1
2 tsp	tahini paste	10 mL
½ tsp	ground cumin	2.5 mL
½ tsp	ground coriander	2.5 mL
½ tsp	ground turmeric	2.5 mL
1 Tbsp	water	15 mL
2 tsp	kosher salt	10 mL
3 Tbsp	olive oil, for pan-frying	45 mL

This is a vegetarian option I have had on the menu periodically; it's my take on falafel. Tahini paste is made from ground sesame seeds and is available from Middle Eastern grocery stores. If I were never to eat meat or fish again, I would surely eat this dish a lot more often. Garnish with a little arugula or a few fresh tomatoes in the summer.

CHICKPEA FRITTERS Place the chickpeas in a large shallow bowl. Crush them with a potato masher or finely chop them with a knife. Add the remaining ingredients (except the olive oil) and stir until combined. You will have a slightly chunky batter. Allow the batter to stand for 30 minutes. (You will have more batter than you need for this recipe. Uncooked batter will keep refrigerated in an airtight container for 1 day. Cooked fritters will keep refrigerated in an airtight container for 2 days.)

continued overleaf...

ROASTED PORTOBELLO MUSHROOMS

2 Tbsp	olive oil	30 mL
4	large portobello mushrooms, stems removed and brown gills scraped out	4
½ cup	unsalted butter, softened	120 mL
	Zest and juice of 1 lemon	
2 cloves	garlic, sliced	2 cloves
4 sprigs	fresh thyme	4 sprigs
1 cup	onion compote (page 156)	250 mL
1 cup	hothouse baby lettuces	240 mL
2 Tbsp	basic vinaigrette (page 236)	30 mL
1 cup	cucumber yogurt (page 236)	250 mL

ROASTED PORTOBELLO MUSHROOMS Preheat the oven to 350°F/175°C. Drizzle the olive oil on a baking sheet and add the mushrooms, undersides up.

In a small bowl, combine the butter, lemon juice and zest until they are well mixed.

Sprinkle the garlic slices over the mushrooms, then top each mushroom with a thyme sprig and ¼ of the butter. Bake for 15 to 20 minutes, until the mushrooms are soft and well cooked. Remove from the oven and allow them to stand on the baking sheet in a warm place.

FINISH CHICKPEA FRITTERS Set a non-stick sauté pan on medium-low heat and add the olive oil. Using a small ladle or a large spoon, drop ¼ cup/60 mL of the fritter batter into the pan. Repeat until you have four mounds. With a spatula, lightly press down on the mounds to flatten them and cook for 3 to 4 minutes per side, or until the fritters are golden brown. Remove the fritters from the pan and allow them to cool on paper towels. Cook more fritters, as desired.

TO SERVE Place a mushroom in the centre of each plate. Top each one with a quarter of the onion compote and a chickpea fritter. In a small bowl, toss the baby lettuces with the vinaigrette. Divide the salad evenly among the plates, placing it over the fritter. Scoop 2 spoonfuls of the cucumber yogurt onto a side of each plate.

WINE Savoury or lightly spicy whites like Grüner Veltliner or Alsace Gewürztraminer will work, or contrast the flavours with a lighter-style, fruity Barbera or Dolcetto.

Parmesan Polenta *with* Braised Greens *and* Fonduta

Serves 4

Polenta is really versatile. This dish can be served as an appetizer and, for variety, the polenta can be grilled as well. There are thousands of combinations that are possible with polenta: from this book, try it with the tomato marmalade (page 238) or in place of the cannelloni with the three cheeses, spinach and tomato sauce (page 72). Paired with New Zealand spinach, an arrowhead-shaped leaf that is heartier than regular spinach, and fonduta, an Italian cheese sauce traditionally made with Fontina cheese, the polenta is a delicious winter dish. Serve it with cooked baby carrots tossed in butter.

PARMESAN POLENTA Lightly oil a shallow 7 × 11 inch/17.5 × 30 cm dish. In a large pot fitted with a lid, combine the milk and water and bring them to a boil on medium heat. Slowly whisk in the polenta, reduce the heat to low and cover and cook for 12 to 15 minutes, or until the polenta no longer looks grainy. Add the butter, Parmesan cheese and a generous pinch of salt. Mix thoroughly and taste, and adjust the seasoning as required.

Pour the polenta into the lightly oiled dish to a depth of ½ inch/1 cm. Refrigerate the polenta until it is cool, about 1 hour. Once the polenta has set, invert the dish onto a cutting board. With a 3-inch/7.5-cm round cookie cutter (or a glass), cut 8 polenta discs and set aside. Will keep refrigerated in an airtight container for up to 3 days.

CHEESE FONDUTA Combine the cream, thyme and bay leaf in a small pot on medium heat. When the mixture comes to a boil, turn off the heat and allow the liquid to infuse for 15 minutes.

continued overleaf...

PARMESAN POLENTA

3 cups	whole milk	750 mL
3 cups	water	750 mL
1 cup	instant polenta	240 mL
⅝ cups	unsalted butter	150 mL
½ cup	grated Parmesan cheese + 1 oz/30g for garnish	120 mL
2 Tbsp	olive oil	30 mL

CHEESE FONDUTA

2 cups	whipping cream	500 mL
1 sprig	fresh thyme	1 sprig
1	bay leaf	1
⅝ cup	grated Parmesan cheese	150 mL
3 oz	soft goat cheese	85 g

Combine the Parmesan and goat cheeses in a medium bowl. Pour the warm cream mixture over the cheeses, whisking constantly until the cheeses have melted and the sauce is well combined. Season lightly with salt, then strain the mixture through a fine-mesh sieve into a clean bowl, discarding the solids, and set aside.

BRAISED GREENS Place the olive oil and shallots in a sauté pan on medium heat and sauté until the shallots are lightly golden, about 3 minutes. Add the greens, garlic and rosemary, tossing well, then pour in the vegetable stock. Cook for 4 to 5 minutes to allow the flavours to develop. Remove from the heat.

FINISH POLENTA Heat the olive oil in a large sauté pan on medium heat. Once the pan is hot, add the polenta rounds (you might have to do this in two batches) and cook them for 4 to 5 minutes on each side, until they are golden brown and heated through. Transfer them to paper towels to drain.

TO SERVE Place a large spoonful of the fonduta on each of 4 large plates. Top the fonduta with a round of polenta, an eighth of the greens and a second piece of polenta. Divide the remaining greens on top of the polenta rounds and generously drizzle each serving with the fonduta. Sprinkle with the Parmesan cheese.

WINE This dish begs for Italian reds, like good-quality Valpolicella, Barbera or Aglianico.

BRAISED GREENS

2 Tbsp	olive oil	30 mL
2	shallots, thinly sliced	2
2 cups	mixed greens (such as rapini, broccolini, New Zealand or regular spinach, kale), picked of heavy stems, washed and dried	480 mL
1 clove	garlic, minced	1 clove
1 tsp	chopped fresh rosemary	5 mL
3 Tbsp	vegetable stock (page 233)	45 mL

Molten Chocolate Cakes *with* Crème Anglaise

Serves 6

CHOCOLATE CAKES

1 cup	unsalted butter, softened	240 mL
8 oz	Valrhona 64% dark chocolate	225 g
2 Tbsp	prepared espresso or strong dark coffee	30 mL
½ cup	white bread flour	120 mL
½ cup	granulated sugar	120 mL
4	eggs	4
4	egg yolks	4

In 1990, when I was a student at the Stratford Chefs School in Ontario, Jean-Georges Vongerichten visited as a guest chef. He made the first warm molten cakes that I had seen, but I remember especially that he invited some Cub Scouts who were standing outside the restaurant to come in and try them. Little did these boys know they were eating what would become one of the most popular chocolate desserts in North America. Here, we provide just the cake recipe, leaving the garnish up to you, although fresh berry coulis or crème anglaise would work equally well.

CHOCOLATE CAKES Grease six ½-cup/125-mL ramekins. Place the butter and the chocolate in a stainless steel bowl over a saucepan of simmering water. Stir frequently with a spoon until the butter and chocolate are melted. Remove from the heat, add the coffee and allow to cool.

Combine the flour, the sugar and a pinch of salt in a medium bowl. With a spatula, blend the dry ingredients into the chocolate mixture in small batches until combined. Mix in the eggs and egg yolks one at a time until they are incorporated. Allow the batter to stand for 15 minutes.

VANILLA CRÈME ANGLAISE Fill a large bowl with ice. Place the egg yolks and the sugar in a medium bowl and whisk together by hand until creamy. In a medium saucepan, combine the cream, milk and vanilla. Bring the cream mixture to a boil on medium heat, then remove it from the heat. Slowly pour the cream into the yolk-sugar mixture, whisking constantly.

Pour the custard back into the saucepan. Reduce the heat to medium and cook, stirring constantly with a rubber spatula to prevent the sauce from sticking to the pot, until the mixture starts to thicken and coats the back of a spoon, 4 to 6 minutes. Be careful not to boil the custard. Remove from the heat and strain the custard through a fine-mesh sieve into a medium bowl, discarding the solids. Place the bowl of custard into the bowl of ice and allow the crème anglaise to cool, stirring occasionally to prevent a skin from forming on top. Will keep refrigerated in an airtight container for up to 4 days.

FINISH CHOCOLATE CAKES Preheat the oven to 400°F/205°C. Stir the batter and divide it evenly among the prepared ramekins, filling them three-quarters full. Bake for 6 to 7 minutes, until the cakes are firmly set on the outside but warm and liquid in the centre. Allow them to stand for 1 minute, then invert the ramekins to unmould the cakes.

TO SERVE Place a dollop of crème anglaise on each of 6 plates and arrange a cake against it. Top with your favourite garnish.

WINE I match this dessert with Banyuls, a fortified French red that is pure magic with chocolate; try the great Banyuls made by Chapoutier.

VANILLA CRÈME ANGLAISE

6	egg yolks	6
½ cup	granulated sugar	120 mL
1⅔ cups	whipping cream	415 mL
½ cup	whole milk	125 mL
1	vanilla bean, pod split and seeds scraped	1

Lemon Tart

Serves 10 to 12 (Yields one 10-inch/25-cm tart)

LEMON SHORTCRUST PASTRY

9 oz	unsalted butter, softened (about 1⅛ cups/270 mL)	255 g
6½ oz	superfine (caster) sugar (about ⅞ cup/ 210 mL)	185 g
1	vanilla bean, seeds scraped and pod discarded	1
2	large eggs, lightly beaten	2
18 oz	all-purpose flour, sifted (about 2¼ cups/540 mL)	510 g
¼ tsp	fine salt	1 mL
1 Tbsp	lemon zest	15 mL
1	egg yolk	1
½ Tbsp	water	7.5 mL

I often feel there is no better way to finish a meal than with a lemon tart. This is a particularly nice one because it is neither too sharp nor too sweet. Also, the pastry is quite versatile and can be used for a variety of fruit-based tarts. This tart is best made in a 10-inch/25-cm round pan that is 1½ inches/3.75 cm deep.

LEMON SHORTCRUST PASTRY Place the butter and sugar in the bowl of an electric mixer fitted with a paddle attachment. Beat at medium speed until smooth and creamy but fluffy, about 8 minutes. Add the vanilla seeds. With the mixer on low speed, gradually add the eggs, turning off the mixer two or three times to scrape down the sides of the bowl.

Lightly flour a clean work surface. Combine the flour, salt and lemon zest in a medium bowl. With the mixer at its lowest speed, add the flour mixture in 3 or 4 batches, being sure to completely incorporate one batch before adding another. Turn off the mixer when the pastry comes together in a crumbly mass.

Transfer the dough to the floured surface and knead it briefly until it becomes smooth. Flatten the dough into a 1-inch/2.5-cm round, tightly wrap it in plastic wrap and refrigerate it for 30 minutes before using.

Preheat the oven to 350°F/175°C. Line a baking sheet with parchment paper and lightly flour a clean work surface. Unwrap the dough, place it on the floured surface and knead it briefly until the dough is soft and pliable but still cool. Keeping the surface lightly dusted with flour, roll the dough evenly into a circle 14 inches/35 cm in diameter and ¼ inch/5 mm thick. Keep the pastry as round and as even as possible.

Set a 10-inch/25-cm flan ring on the baking sheet. Wrap the pastry round onto a rolling pin and transfer it to the flan ring, unrolling it and gently pressing the pastry into the ring, and allowing any excess dough to hang over the edge of the mould (it will be trimmed off later). Refrigerate the pastry for 10 minutes.

Blind-bake the pastry by lining the tart shell with aluminum foil, filling it with baking beans or pie weights and baking it for 15 to 20 minutes, until the edges are golden brown. Gently remove the baking beans (or pie weights) and the aluminum foil and return the pan to the oven for another 6 to 8 minutes until the base of the tart shell is pale gold. Remove from the oven and allow the pastry to cool to room temperature.

continued overleaf...

LEMON FILLING

12	large eggs	12
2½ cups	granulated sugar	600 mL
	Juice of 8 lemons	
	Zest of 4 lemons	
1⅓ cups	whipping cream	330 mL
¼ cup	icing sugar, for garnish	60 mL
1 recipe	raspberry coulis (page 98), for garnish	1 recipe

LEMON FILLING In a large bowl, whisk together the eggs and the granulated sugar until well combined. Add the lemon juice and continue whisking until it is thoroughly combined. Strain the mixture through a fine-mesh sieve into a clean bowl. Stir in the lemon zest.

Pour the cream into the bowl of an electric mixer and beat at low speed until it just forms soft peaks, then use a spatula to fold it into the lemon mixture. Refrigerate the filling for 30 minutes.

FINISH LEMON TART Preheat the oven to 350°F/175°C. Combine the egg yolk, the water and a small pinch of salt in a bowl and whisk until well blended. With a pastry brush, paint this egg wash over the blind-baked tart shell.

Stir the tart filling to re-emulsify it. Place the tart shell into the oven, then pour the filling directly into the pastry. Reduce the heat to 325°F/160°C and bake for 20 minutes, turning the tart gently if required to cook it evenly. Reduce the heat to 300°F/150°C and bake for 15 minutes more. Turn off the oven and continue baking the tart until the filling is barely wobbly when jiggled, about 15 more minutes.

Remove the tart from the oven and, using a sharp knife, trim the overhanging crust. Allow the tart to cool to room temperature before unmoulding and slicing.

TO SERVE Fill a small bowl with hot water. Dip a sharp knife in the water, then wipe it with a towel before each slice to ensure a clean cut. Slice the lemon tart into 10 or 12 slices. Dust each slice with icing sugar and serve with raspberry coulis.

WINE Late-harvest Riesling from Germany, Austria or B.C. would be delicious.

Pineapple Upside-down "Tart"

Serves 6

1 ¼ cups	granulated sugar	300 mL
½ cup	dark rum	125 mL
1	vanilla bean, seeds scraped and pod discarded	1
1	large Hawaiian Gold pineapple	1
1 recipe	pâte sablé (page 98)	1 recipe
1 recipe	sour cream ice cream (page 90), for garnish	1 recipe

This dessert is a new take on a tarte Tatin, which is traditionally made with apples, and it is great in the winter because pineapples are at their best. Pineapples have a firm texture that really holds up to cooking, and the sablé dough is versatile enough to be used for tarts as well as for cookies. When you prepare this pastry, be sure to make extra as it generally freezes well. At the restaurant, we like to garnish this tart with an oven-dried pineapple chip (page 240).

SET SIX 4-INCH/10-CM ramekins on a baking sheet. Place the sugar in a medium saucepan and moisten it with 1 cup/250 mL water. Heat the sugar on medium-high heat, swirling the pan to cook the sugar evenly, until it starts to brown, about 10 minutes. Remove the caramel from the heat and carefully add the rum and the vanilla (be careful, as the sugar will spit). Turn down the heat to medium and return the pan to the heat until the caramel melts again, about 5 minutes, then pour the caramel evenly into the 6 ramekins. Allow the caramel to cool to room temperature.

Using a sharp knife, trim the skin off the pineapple and discard it. Cut the fruit widthwise into slices 1 inch/2.5 cm thick. Using a 3-inch/7.5-cm pastry cutter or a sharp knife, cut the pineapple slices into 6 even circles. Use a tiny cutter to remove the tough core at the centre of each slice. (The slices will resemble doughnuts.) Place the slices in the prepared ramekins.

continued overleaf…

Preheat the oven to 350°F/175°C. Line a baking sheet with parchment paper and lightly flour a clean work surface. Unwrap the sablé dough and roll it to a ¼-inch/5-mm thickness. Using a round cutter with a 3 ½-inch/8-cm diameter or a sharp knife, cut out 6 discs. Gently transfer the rounds to the baking sheet and refrigerate for 10 minutes.

Place the chilled rounds into the oven and bake until golden brown (10 to 12 minutes). Remove the sablé discs from the oven. Immediately trim them using a round cutter with a 3-inch/7.5-cm diameter or a knife to make the sablé cookies the same size as the prepared pineapple rings. Allow the sablé cookies to cool to room temperature.

Reduce the oven temperature to 385°F/195°C. Bake the pineapple slices in the ramekins until the caramelized sugar is bubbling and the pineapple begins to soften, about 10 to 15 minutes. If the pineapple needs more time to cook, reduce the heat to 355°F/180°C; otherwise, the caramelized sugar will start to burn. Remove the ramekins from the oven and cool for 5 minutes. Carefully pour off and reserve half of the liquid from each ramekin. Leaving the pineapple rings in the ramekins, gently press a sablé disc on to the top of each one. Return the ramekins to the oven, and heat briefly, about 5 minutes.

TO SERVE Carefully invert a freshly baked pineapple tart onto the middle of each dessert plate. Spoon a small amount of the reserved cooking liquid over each one. Place a scoop of sour cream ice cream directly on top of each pineapple tart. Serve warm.

WINE An Australian Muscat liqueur is delicious, or try some Austrian Beerenauslese.

Black Forest Cake *with* Brandied-Cherry Ice Cream

Serves 10 to 12 (Yields one 10-inch/25-cm cake)

BRANDIED-CHERRY ICE CREAM

6	large egg yolks	6
½ cup	granulated sugar	120 mL
1½ cups	whipping cream	375 mL
½ cup	whole milk	125 mL
1	vanilla bean, pod split and seeds scraped	1
½ cup	brandied cherries (page 239)	120 mL
½ cup	coarsely chopped dark chocolate or dark chocolate chips	120 mL

At Araxi, we make individual Black Forest cakes using small metal ring moulds and we spray them with melted chocolate loaded into a paint gun to give them a nice finished texture. We have adapted this recipe to make one large cake with a traditional garnish.

Time is of the essence when preparing this cake. Once the mousses are prepared, they start to set rather quickly. The best method is to prepare the dark chocolate mousse first, build the bottom layer of the cake and then proceed with the white chocolate–kirsch mousse and the second layer of the cake. Use gelatin leaves rather than powder, for more consistent results.

BRANDIED-CHERRY ICE CREAM Fill a large bowl with ice. Place the egg yolks and sugar in a large bowl and whisk by hand until light and creamy. In a large saucepan, combine the cream, milk, vanilla seeds and vanilla pod. Bring the cream mixture to a boil on medium heat, then remove it from the heat. Slowly pour the cream into the yolk-sugar mixture, stirring constantly.

Pour the custard back into the saucepan. Reduce the heat to medium and cook, stirring constantly with a heat-resistant rubber spatula, until the mixture starts to thicken and coats the back of the spatula, 4 to 6 minutes. Be careful not to boil the custard. Remove from the heat and strain the custard through a fine-mesh sieve into a medium bowl, discarding the solids. Place the bowl of custard into the bowl of ice and allow the custard to cool, stirring occasionally to prevent a skin from forming on top. Cover tightly with plastic wrap and refrigerate for at least 12 hours.

Place the custard in an ice cream maker and churn it according to the manufacturer's instructions. Fold in the brandied cherries and the chocolate once you remove the

FLOURLESS CHOCOLATE CAKE

11½ oz	egg yolks (about 11)	320 g
11½ oz	whipping cream (about 1½ cups/ 375 mL)	320 g
5½ oz	cocoa powder, sifted (about ⅝ cup/150 mL)	150 g
14 oz	egg whites (about 15)	400 g
14 oz	granulated sugar (about 1⅔ cups/ 400 mL)	400 g
3 cups	brandied cherries (page 239), for garnish	700 mL
4 oz	dark chocolate (64% cocoa), for garnish	115 g

ice cream from the machine. Will keep frozen in an air-tight container for up to 4 days. Makes about 4 cups/1 L of ice cream.

FLOURLESS CHOCOLATE CAKE Preheat the oven to 365°F/185°C. Lightly grease two 10-inch/25-cm spring-form pans and line them with parchment paper.

Combine the egg yolks, cream and cocoa powder in the bowl of an electric mixer fitted with a paddle attachment. Mix at the lowest speed until the ingredients just come together, about 3 minutes. Increase the speed to medium and process until you have a smooth and lump-free cocoa paste, 2 to 3 minutes. Transfer this paste to a large clean bowl and set aside.

continued overleaf...

KIRSCH SYRUP

3½ Tbsp or to taste	kirsch (cherry brandy)	50 mL or to taste
1 cup	simple syrup (page 239)	250 mL

DARK CHOCOLATE MOUSSE

4 oz	Valrhona dark chocolate (64% cocoa)	115 g
2	egg yolks	2
2 Tbsp	granulated sugar	30 mL
1⅔ cups	whipping cream	415 mL

Thoroughly wash and dry the mixer's bowl and fit the mixer with a whisk attachment. Place the egg whites and sugar in the bowl and process at medium speed until the sugar is roughly distributed. Increase to the highest speed and whip the mixture until it forms soft peaks, about 6 minutes.

Using a spatula, fold a third of this meringue into the cocoa paste and mix until smooth. Gently fold in the remaining meringue and mix until fully combined. Divide the cake batter evenly between the 2 pans, using a palette knife to smooth the surface of the cake batter. Bake for 10 minutes, then rotate the cake pans to ensure even cooking and bake for about 5 minutes more, or until the cake springs back when pressed but is still moist. Transfer the pans to wire racks to cool. Remove the pans but leave the parchment paper attached to the cakes.

KIRSCH SYRUP In a small bowl, stir the kirsch into the simple syrup until well mixed. Set aside.

DARK CHOCOLATE MOUSSE Melt the chocolate in a stainless steel bowl set over a saucepan of gently simmering water. Set aside.

In a second stainless steel bowl, whisk together the egg yolks, sugar and 3½ Tbsp/50 mL of the cream. Place this bowl over the saucepan of simmering water and whisk until the mixture is pale yellow and fluffy, about 5 minutes. Remove the bowl from the heat and stir in the melted chocolate. Allow this chocolate mixture to cool to room temperature.

In the bowl of an electric mixer fitted with a whisk attachment, whip the remaining cream at medium speed until it forms soft peaks, about 5 minutes. Using a spatula, fold half of the whipped cream into the chocolate mixture. Gently fold in the remaining whipped cream, ensuring that the mousse is fully mixed. Spoon the mousse into a piping bag fitted with a wide nozzle.

WHITE CHOCOLATE-KIRSCH MOUSSE Melt the white chocolate in a stainless steel bowl over a saucepan of gently simmering water. Set aside. Place the gelatin in a small bowl and add enough cold water to cover the leaves completely. Allow to soak for 3 minutes.

Combine the sugar, the vanilla and ½ cup/125 mL of the cream in a small saucepan. Bring the mixture to a boil on medium heat and boil until the sugar dissolves, about 3 minutes. Remove the gelatin from the water, squeezing out any excess water, and place the leaves in a large bowl. Carefully pour the hot cream mixture over the gelatin, whisking to completely dissolve it. Stir in the melted white chocolate and whisk in the kirsch. Allow this chocolate mixture to cool to room temperature.

In the bowl of an electric mixer fitted with a whisk attachment, whip the remaining cream at medium speed until it forms soft peaks, about 4 minutes. Using a spatula, fold a third of the whipped cream into the chocolate mixture. Gently fold in the remaining whipped cream, ensuring that the mousse is fully mixed. Spoon the mousse into a piping bag fitted with a wide nozzle.

continued overleaf...

WHITE CHOCOLATE-KIRSCH MOUSSE

5 ½ oz	white chocolate	155 g
4 leaves	gelatin	4 leaves
2 Tbsp	granulated sugar	30 mL
1	vanilla bean, seeds scraped and pod discarded	1
3 cups	whipping cream	750 mL
⅓ cup + 1 tsp	kirsch (cherry brandy)	85 mL

SWEETENED WHIPPED CREAM

1 cup	whipping cream	250 mL
1 tsp	granulated sugar	5 mL
1	vanilla bean, seeds scraped and pod discarded	1

SWEETENED WHIPPED CREAM Combine the cream, sugar and vanilla in the bowl of an electric mixer fitted with a whisk attachment. Beat at medium speed for 4 minutes, or until the cream forms stiff peaks.

FINISH BLACK FOREST CAKE Lightly grease and line a deep 10-inch/25-cm springform pan with parchment paper. Place one of the cakes in the pan and brush it with half of the kirsch syrup. Pipe the dark chocolate mousse on top of the cake and use a palette knife to spread it into an even layer. Sprinkle 1 cup/240 mL of the brandied cherries evenly over the mousse. Set the second cake on top, pressing it down firmly. Pour the remaining half of the kirsch syrup over the second cake. Pipe half of the white chocolate–kirsch mousse onto the cake, cover it with another 1 cup/240 mL of the brandied cherries, then top it with the remaining white chocolate mousse. Smooth the surface, then refrigerate the cake for at least 8 hours.

Remove the springform pan and gently peel off and discard the paper. Using a spatula, spread the sweetened whipped cream along the sides of the cake. Smooth the top of the cake again. Using a rasp, grate the dark chocolate over the top of the cake, completely covering it.

TO SERVE Fill a small bowl with hot water. Dip a sharp knife in the water, then wipe it with a towel before each slice to ensure a clean cut. Slice the Black Forest cake into 10 or 12 slices. Serve each slice with a scoop of brandied-cherry ice cream topped with a few brandied cherries.

WINE Good choices include LBV port, Banyuls or some PX sherry.

Chocolate Caramel Pots de Crème
with Milk Chocolate–Almond Biscotti

Serves 6

A simple dessert with a simple garnish, these pots de crème are quite rich and almost pudding-like. Serve them after a light meal. Both the pots de crème and the biscotti keep quite well, so if you are entertaining, consider this dessert—or other pots de crème, panna cottas or crèmes caramel—because you can prepare it ahead of time. For an elegant presentation, serve it with a chocolate tuile.

POTS DE CRÈME Preheat the oven to 310°F/155°C. Place six 5-oz/140-g ramekins in a deep ovenproof dish that is taller than the ramekins.

Melt the chocolate in a stainless steel bowl over a saucepan filled one-quarter full of gently simmering water. Be sure that the bowl does not touch the water. Keep warm.

Combine the eggs and egg yolks in a large bowl, whisking them just until smooth. Set aside. Combine the milk, cream and vanilla and set aside.

Place the sugar in a deep saucepan, add the water and stir until the water is thoroughly incorporated. With a small pastry brush dipped in water, brush the sides of the pot to remove any sugar crystals. Cook the sugar over medium-high heat, without stirring, until it caramelizes to a deep golden brown, about 8 minutes. Remove the pot from the heat and carefully pour the caramelized sugar into the milk mixture. The sugar will spit and sizzle. Return the pot to the heat and bring the mixture to a gentle boil, then stir with a whisk to fully dissolve the caramelized sugar. Turn off the heat. Whisk in the melted chocolate until it is fully incorporated.

continued overleaf...

POTS DE CRÈME

5 oz	dark chocolate (64% cocoa)	140 g
2	large eggs	2
6	egg yolks	6
1½ cups	whole milk	375 mL
1½ cups	whipping cream	375 mL
1	vanilla bean, pod split and seeds scraped	1
1 cup	granulated sugar	240 mL
¼ cup	water	60 mL
1 cup	whipped cream, for garnish	240 mL

MILK CHOCOLATE–ALMOND BISCOTTI

¼ cup	vegetable oil	60 mL
¼ cup	honey	60 mL
¼ cup	granulated sugar	60 mL
½	vanilla bean, seeds scraped and pod discarded	½
1	large egg	1
1 cup	all-purpose flour	240 mL
½ tsp	baking powder	2.5 mL
¼ tsp	baking soda	1 mL
¼ tsp	salt	1 mL
¾ cup	roughly chopped raw almonds	180 mL
½ cup	roughly chopped milk chocolate	120 mL

Pour the hot chocolate mixture over the beaten eggs, whisking constantly. Strain the mixture through a fine-mesh sieve, discarding any solids, and divide it evenly among the ramekins. Fill the ovenproof dish holding the ramekins with hot water to ½ inch/1 cm below the tops of the ramekins. Cover the dish with aluminum foil and gently transfer it to the oven. Bake for about 20 minutes, carefully rotating the dish after about 10 minutes to ensure even cooking. To check for doneness, carefully remove the foil (watch out for the hot steam) and gently shake the baking dish; the custards should wiggle like jelly but not be liquid in appearance. When the pots de crème are done, remove the ramekins from the dish and refrigerate them for 45 minutes, until chilled. Will keep refrigerated in an airtight container for up to 4 days.

MILK CHOCOLATE–ALMOND BISCOTTI Combine the vegetable oil, honey, sugar, vanilla and egg in a large bowl, whisking until the ingredients are fully combined.

In a separate bowl, sift together the flour, baking powder, baking soda and salt. Using a rubber spatula, stir the dry ingredients into the wet mixture. Add the almonds and chocolate and mix until well combined. Refrigerate the biscotti dough for about 2 hours, or until well chilled.

continued overleaf...

Preheat the oven to 320°F/160°C. Line a baking sheet with parchment paper and lightly flour a clean work surface. Place a second baking sheet under the first one to prevent the bottoms of the biscotti from scorching. Divide the dough into 2 equal parts. Hand-roll each piece of dough into a log about 10 inches/25 cm long and 1½ inches/3.5 cm in diameter. Place the logs on the baking sheet and bake them for 10 minutes. Reduce the temperature to 290°F/145°C and bake for 10 to 12 minutes more, until they are golden brown and springy to the touch. Remove the logs from the oven and allow them to cool for 5 minutes.

Reduce the oven temperature further, to 200°F/95°C. Cut each log crosswise into ½-inch/1-cm rounds and arrange them on the baking sheet. Bake until the biscotti are dry and lightly brown on top, about 8 minutes.

TO SERVE Place a ramekin on each of 6 individual plates. Garnish each serving with a dollop of freshly whipped cream and three biscotti.

WINE Enjoy this dessert with an older tawny port, or an Australian Muscat liqueur or tawny such as a Penfolds Grandfather.

Mascarpone Cheesecake *with* Honey-Caramel Apples *and* Almond Praline

Serves 8 to 10 (Yields one 10-inch/25-cm cake)

ALMOND PRALINE

1 cup	whole natural almonds	240 mL
¾ cup	granulated sugar	180 mL

MASCARPONE CHEESECAKE

8 oz	mascarpone cheese, room temperature	225 g
11¼ oz	cream cheese, room temperature	320 g
⅝ cup	granulated sugar	150 mL
1	vanilla bean, seeds scraped and pod discarded	1
5	large eggs	5
3	egg yolks	5
⅓ cup	whipping cream	80 mL
2 cups	vanilla crème anglaise (page 208), for garnish	500 mL

The mascarpone cheese makes this cheesecake a little lighter than most, but quite creamy at the same time. We use Pink Lady, Granny Smith or Cox's Orange Pippin apples for this recipe because they are firm, tangy and keep their shape and texture when cooked. You can substitute hazelnuts, walnuts or pecans for the almonds in the praline—or, if you want, try a regular graham cracker crust. At Araxi, we prepare individual portions, but the whole cake recipe here is just as delicious and easier to make. We garnish them with oven-dried apple chips (page 240) to provide a contrast in texture and to heighten the apple flavour.

ALMOND PRALINE Preheat the oven to 350°F/175°C. Line a baking sheet with parchment paper. Arrange the almonds on the baking sheet and toast until very lightly browned, 8 to 10 minutes. Remove from the oven and allow the nuts to cool on the baking sheet.

In a small pot, combine the sugar with just enough water to moisten it evenly (about ¼ cup/60 mL). Heat the sugar on medium heat, without stirring, until it is caramelized and light amber, about 10 minutes. Pour this syrup over the almonds and stir gently until the nuts are evenly coated. Allow the praline to cool completely, then grind it in batches in a food processor until you have a fine powder.

MASCARPONE CHEESECAKE Preheat the oven to 300°F/150°C. Tightly wrap the bottom of a 10-inch/25-cm diameter bottomless metal ring mould with aluminum foil. Place the mould into a large roasting pan. Place the roasting pan on a baking sheet.

continued overleaf...

HONEY-CARAMEL APPLES

8	large Granny Smith apples or other firm cooking apples	8
	Juice of 1 lemon	
½ cup	granulated sugar	120 mL
1	vanilla bean, pod split and seeds scraped	1
¾ cup	Denman Island apple juice or similar organic apple juice	185 mL
¼ cup	Golden Cariboo honey or similar unpasteurized liquid honey	60 mL

In the bowl of an electric mixer fitted with a paddle attachment, combine the mascarpone and cream cheeses with the sugar and vanilla. Mix on medium speed until the cheeses are well blended and the sugar is dissolved, about 5 minutes.

In a separate bowl, whisk together the eggs, egg yolks and cream. With the motor running at low speed, add the egg mixture to the cheese mixture. Scraping down the sides of the bowl 2 or 3 times, mix until the batter is just combined and smooth, about 3 minutes total. Strain the batter through a fine-mesh sieve into the prepared ring mould. Discard the solids. Fill the roasting pan with enough hot water to reach halfway up the side of the ring mould.

Bake for 15 minutes, then turn the baking sheet around and lower the temperature to 285°C/140°C. Bake for 10 to 15 minutes more, or until a dry knife inserted in the centre of the cake comes out clean. Remove the ring mould from the water bath. Refrigerate the cheesecake for 2 hours or until chilled.

Line a cake platter or a large plate with parchment paper. Carefully remove the aluminum foil from the bottom of the cheesecake, then gently transfer the cheesecake to the platter (or plate). Dip a knife in hot water, then run it around the edges of the mould to loosen the filling. Gently slide the mould up and away from the cheesecake.

HONEY-CARAMEL APPLES Peel and core the apples, then cut them into ¼-inch/5-mm slices. Place the apple slices in a large bowl and toss them with the lemon juice to prevent oxidization.

In a large sauté pan on medium heat, cook the sugar until it turns a golden brown, about 4 minutes. Add the apples to the pan, then stir in the vanilla seeds and pod. Deglaze the pan with the apple juice and honey, then sauté the apples, stirring frequently, until the liquid is reduced and the apple slices are slightly translucent, about 15 minutes. (If the pan dries out too quickly, add ¼ cup/60 mL more apple juice.) Remove the apples from the heat and transfer them to a stainless steel bowl. Allow the mixture to cool to room temperature, then discard the vanilla pod. Set aside.

FINISH CHEESECAKE Gently sift half of the almond praline onto a clean work surface, and shape it into a circle 11 inches/27.5 cm in diameter. Carefully place the cheesecake onto the praline and press gently on the cake to coat the bottom of it. Using two lifters, transfer the cheesecake to a large cake platter or serving plate.

Cut a sheet of parchment paper into a 10-inch/25-cm circle. Slide the ring mould back around the cake, then fan the apple slices in a circle on the top of the cheesecake, ensuring that they reach right to the edge. Place the parchment paper over the apples and lightly press it down with your hands to set the apples onto the cheesecake. Remove the parchment paper and the ring mould. Using a plastic scraper, coat the sides of the cheesecake with the remaining almond praline.

TO SERVE Using a sharp knife dipped in hot water and then dried, slice the cake into individual servings. Serve with generous spoonfuls of vanilla crème anglaise.

WINE I pair this dish with fabulous apple ice cider from Domaine Pinnacle in Quebec. It is widely available, but if you can't find it, sip some B.C. late-harvest Riesling.

Basics

Clarified Butter

Yields 1 ½ cups/355 mL

1 lb	unsalted butter	454 g

Clarified butter is preferred in many recipes because it has a higher smoke point than regular butter, so it can be used to cook at higher temperatures—for instance, when frying or sautéing.

MELT THE BUTTER in a small saucepan on low heat. Simmer for 8 to 10 minutes, skimming the foam off the top to remove any impurities. Remove from the heat and allow the solids to settle to the bottom of the pot. Pour the butter through a fine-mesh sieve or a coffee filter into a clean bowl, discarding any solids. Will keep refrigerated in an airtight container for up to 10 days.

Sweet Pickling Brine

Yields 4 cups/1 L

3 cups	water	750 mL
2 cups	granulated sugar	480 mL
1 cup	white wine vinegar	250 mL
1 Tbsp	pickling spice	15 mL

This pickling liquid keeps very well, so make lots and use it to pickle vegetables such as daikon radishes, carrots or crosnes. The pickling spice I use contains allspice, coriander seeds, bay leaf, cloves and fennel seeds, but other spices work equally well.

COMBINE ALL OF the ingredients in a small saucepan and bring to a boil on medium heat. Turn off the heat and allow the mixture to cool. Before using, strain the brine through a fine-mesh sieve into a clean bowl, discarding the pickling spice. Will keep refrigerated in an airtight container for 2 to 3 weeks.

Vegetable Nage *and* Stock

Yields 10 cups/2.5 L

5	carrots, sliced	5
8	shallots, sliced	8
4 stalks	celery, sliced	4 stalks
3 cloves	garlic, sliced	3 cloves
2	onions, sliced	2
4	whole star anise	4
1	large fennel bulb, sliced	1
3	bay leaves	3
8	coriander seeds	8
8 cups	water	2 L
1 cup	white wine	250 mL

There are a lot of vegetables in this recipe because the nage is a very well flavoured broth. Use this basic nage recipe to make a good vegetable stock by adding an additional 16 cups/ 4 L of water.

IN A LARGE stockpot, combine all of the ingredients except the wine. Bring to a boil on medium-high heat, then reduce the heat to low and simmer gently for 20 minutes. Remove from the heat, stir in the white wine and refrigerate for 45 minutes, or until chilled. Strain the nage through a fine-mesh sieve into a clean bowl, discarding any solids. Will keep refrigerated in an airtight container for up to 5 days or frozen for up to 3 weeks.

Fish Stock

Yields 14 cups/3.5 L

3 Tbsp	butter	45 mL
2	leeks, white parts only, sliced	2
1	carrot, chopped	1
2 stalks	celery, chopped	2 stalks
1 cup	white wine	250 mL
5 lbs	white fish bones, rinsed in cold water	2.25 kg
16 cups	water	4 L
1	bay leaf	1
1 tsp	white peppercorns	5 mL
2 sprigs	fresh parsley	2 sprigs
1	lemon, sliced	1

IN A LARGE stockpot, melt the butter on low heat. Add the leeks, carrots and celery and sauté for 7 to 8 minutes to soften the vegetables and release the flavours. Pour in the white wine, cook for 2 minutes, then add the fish bones, water, bay leaf, peppercorns and parsley. Increase the heat to medium and when the stock almost comes to a boil, reduce the heat to low and simmer for 20 minutes, frequently skimming the surface with a slotted spoon to remove any impurities. Remove the stock from the heat, add the lemon and allow it to stand for 5 minutes. Strain the stock through a fine-mesh sieve or a cheesecloth into a clean bowl, discarding any solids. Allow the stock to cool. Will keep refrigerated in an airtight container for up to 3 days or frozen for up to 3 weeks.

Veal Stock

Yields 18 cups/4.5 L

10 lbs	meaty veal bones (such as knuckles, skin and neck)	4.5 kg
2	pig's feet (trotters)	2
16 to 20 cups	water, cold	4 to 5 L
¼ cup	grapeseed oil	60 mL
2	onions, chopped	2
3	large carrots, chopped	3
4 stalks	celery, chopped	4 stalks
3 cloves	garlic	3 cloves
3 cups	red wine	750 mL
½ cup	tomato paste	120 mL
2 cups	canned tomatoes, juice reserved	480 mL
10	black peppercorns	10
1	bay leaf	1
2 sprigs	fresh parsley	2 sprigs

Pig's feet, also known as trotters, are available from your local butcher.

PREHEAT THE OVEN to 375°F/190°C. Place the veal bones and pig's feet in a deep roasting pan and roast for 40 to 45 minutes. Turn the bones and roast them for another 45 minutes to 1 hour, or until they are deep brown and the oils are cooked out. Transfer the bones and pig's feet to a large stockpot, pouring off and discarding any fat. Cover the bones with cold water until just covered and bring to a boil on high heat, then reduce the heat to medium and allow to simmer, skimming the surface frequently with a slotted spoon to remove any fat and foam.

In a separate saucepan, heat the grapeseed oil on medium-high heat and add the onions, carrots, celery and garlic and sauté until nicely browned, about 20 minutes. Pour in the red wine and cook until the wine has reduced by two-thirds, about 15 minutes. Stir in the tomato paste and cook for 5 minutes, then add the tomatoes and cook for 10 minutes. Add this vegetable mixture to the veal bones. The liquid should now be 2 to 3 inches/5 to 7.5 cm above the bones.

Add the peppercorns, bay leaf and parsley, reduce the heat to low and simmer for 6 to 8 hours. Using a slotted spoon, skim off and discard the fat when it accumulates. Strain the stock through a fine-mesh sieve or a cheesecloth into a clean bowl. Refrigerate for 2 hours, until chilled. Will keep refrigerated in an airtight container for up to 1 week or frozen for up to 1 month.

Veal Demi-glace

Yields 2 cups/500 mL

4 cups	veal stock (page 234)	1 L

I use this demi-glace to make sauces or enhance braised dishes.

IN A SMALL saucepan, bring the veal stock to a boil on high heat. Reduce the heat to medium and simmer until the stock is reduced by half, about 20 minutes. Allow to cool to room temperature. Will keep refrigerated in an airtight container for up to 1 week or frozen for up to 1 month.

Chicken Stock

Yields 9 to 10 cups/2.25 to 2.5 L

5 lbs	chicken bones (such as necks, wings and backs)	2.25 kg
1	large carrot, chopped	1
2 stalks	celery, chopped	2 stalks
1	onion, chopped	1
1 clove	garlic, sliced	1 clove
1 sprig	fresh thyme	1 sprig
1	bay leaf	1
5	black peppercorns	5

RINSE THE CHICKEN bones under cold water, then place them in a large stockpot and cover with water. Bring to a boil on high heat, then remove from the heat and pour off the cloudy water. Add all of the remaining ingredients and about 10 cups/2.5 L of cold water, or enough to cover the bones. Bring to a boil on medium heat, then reduce the heat to low and simmer for about 2 hours, skimming the top with a slotted spoon to remove the fat. Strain the stock through a fine-mesh sieve or a cheesecloth into a clean bowl. Allow the stock to cool. Will keep refrigerated in an airtight container for up to 5 days or frozen for up to 1 month.

Basil Oil

Yields 1 cup/250 mL

½ cup	sliced leeks, dark green tops only	120 mL
3 cups	fresh basil	720 mL
1 cup	grapeseed oil	250 mL

This oil works well with fish dishes or can be used to make a flavoured mayonnaise. Chives, parsley or tarragon can also be prepared using this method.

FILL A LARGE bowl with ice water. Bring a medium pot of water to a boil on high heat. Add the leeks and cook for 4 to 5 minutes, or until soft. Add the basil and cook for 20 seconds. Using a slotted spoon, transfer the leeks and basil to the ice water to stop the cooking and preserve their colour.

Drain the leeks and basil in a colander and squeeze out any excess moisture. Place the vegetables in a blender with the grapeseed oil and purée at high speed until smooth. Refrigerate for 12 hours, then strain the oil through a fine-mesh sieve or a coffee filter into a clean bowl. Will keep refrigerated in an airtight container for up to 3 days.

Basic Vinaigrette

Yields 3 ¾ cups/930 mL

3 cups	extra-virgin olive oil	750 mL
¾ cup	red wine vinegar	185 mL
1 tsp	kosher salt	5 mL

IN A LARGE bowl, whisk together all of the ingredients with a pinch of freshly ground pepper. Will keep refrigerated in an airtight container for up to 2 weeks.

Lemon Butter

Yields 1 cup/240 mL

1 cup	unsalted butter, at room temperature	240 mL
	Juice of 2 lemons	
	Zest of 1 lemon	
1	small hot red chili pepper, minced	1
1 Tbsp	chopped fresh parsley	15 mL
1 tsp	chopped fresh cilantro	5 mL

CUT AN 11 × 18-inch/30 × 45-cm sheet of parchment paper. Place all of the ingredients in a large bowl, add a pinch of kosher salt and mix well to combine. Position the butter in the middle of the parchment paper and shape it into a log. Fold the bottom of the parchment paper over the butter, tuck in the sides of the paper like an envelope, then roll the paper away from you, encasing the butter in the parchment paper. Will keep refrigerated for up to 5 days or frozen for up to 2 weeks.

Cucumber Yogurt

Yields 3 cups/750 mL

2	large English cucumbers, peeled and seeded	2
1 Tbsp	salt	15 mL
2 cups	plain yogurt	500 mL
2 cloves	garlic, finely minced	2 cloves
2 Tbsp	olive oil	30 mL
	Juice of 1 lemon	
1 Tbsp	finely chopped fresh mint	15 mL

This yogurt works well with grilled meats like kebabs or as a condiment with spicy Indian dishes.

CUT THE CUCUMBERS into ¼-inch/5-mm slices and place them in a large colander set over a bowl. Sprinkle the slices with the salt and allow to stand for at least 30 minutes.

Place a fine-mesh sieve over a clean bowl, add the yogurt and allow it to stand for 45 minutes so any excess moisture drains out.

Rinse the cucumber slices under running water and pat them dry. Combine the cucumber, strained yogurt, garlic, olive oil, lemon juice and mint in a blender, then purée at high speed until the mixture has the consistency of relish, about 2 minutes. Season with salt and pepper and more lemon juice, if needed. Will keep refrigerated in an airtight container for up to 3 days.

Citrus-Soy Dressing

Yields 2 ¼ cups/560 mL

1 ¼ cups	soy sauce	315 mL
⅞ cup	orange juice	220 mL
⅓ cup	water	80 mL

PLACE ALL OF the ingredients in a medium bowl and whisk until blended. Strain the dressing through a fine-mesh sieve or a cheesecloth into a clean bowl. Refrigerate for 45 minutes, until chilled. Will keep refrigerated in an airtight container for up to 1 week.

Ponzu Sauce

Yields 1 ⅔ cups/415 mL

½ cup	rice wine vinegar	125 mL
⅓ cup	soy sauce	80 mL
⅓ cup	orange juice	80 mL
½ cup	granulated sugar	120 mL
4 tsp	yuzu juice	20 mL

This sauce is great with raw or seared seafood dishes. Yuzu juice is a citrus juice that is available from Japanese grocery stores. If it is not available, substitute 2 parts lemon juice to 1 part lime juice.

PLACE ALL OF the ingredients in a medium bowl and whisk until blended. Strain the sauce through a fine-mesh sieve or a cheesecloth into a clean bowl. Refrigerate for 45 minutes, until chilled. Will keep refrigerated in an airtight container for up to 1 week.

Mustard Sauce

Yields 2 cups/500 mL

2 Tbsp	grapeseed oil	30 mL
4	shallots, sliced	4
1 clove	garlic, sliced	1 clove
2 Tbsp	grainy mustard	30 mL
1 tsp	Dijon mustard	5 mL
½ cup	port	125 mL
3 cups	veal demi-glace (page 234)	750 mL

This sauce works well with roasted meats, sausages and hearty fish, like sturgeon.

HEAT THE GRAPESEED oil in a small saucepan on medium heat. Add the shallots and garlic and sauté until softened and lightly coloured, about 3 minutes. Add the grainy and Dijon mustards and cook for 2 minutes, then pour in the port and allow it to reduce to almost a syrup, about 4 minutes. Add the veal demi-glace and bring the mixture to a boil. Reduce the heat to low and simmer until the sauce coats the back of a spoon, about 6 minutes. Will keep refrigerated in an airtight container for up to 1 week.

Tomato Marmalade

Yields 2 cups/500 mL

3 Tbsp	olive oil	45 mL
1	red jalapeño pepper, thinly sliced	1
5	shallots, thinly sliced	5
2 cloves	garlic, sliced	2 cloves
½-inch piece	fresh ginger, peeled and thinly sliced	1-cm piece
½ cup	brown sugar	120 mL
½ stick	cinnamon	½ stick
¼ cup	sherry vinegar	60 mL
2 Tbsp	tomato paste	30 mL
3 cups	canned tomatoes, drained, or fresh tomatoes, peeled and cored	750 mL

At Araxi, we regularly use this condiment on our burgers, and to enhance the flavour of braised pork bellies or crispy zucchini blossoms.

COMBINE THE OLIVE oil, jalapeño peppers, shallots, garlic and ginger in a medium saucepan on medium heat. Sauté for 8 to 10 minutes, until the vegetables are softened and lightly golden brown. Add the brown sugar, cinnamon and sherry vinegar and cook for 5 minutes, until the mixture is syrupy. Stir in the tomato paste and cook the sauce for 5 minutes. Add the tomatoes and bring the sauce to a boil. Reduce the heat to low and simmer for 25 to 30 minutes, until the sauce thickens to an almost jamlike consistency. Transfer the marmalade to a baking sheet and refrigerate it until cool, about 45 minutes.

Before serving, remove and discard the cinnamon stick. Spoon the marmalade onto a clean work surface and, using a sharp knife, chop it to create a chunky texture. Do not purée the marmalade. Will keep refrigerated in an airtight container for 4 to 5 days.

Tapenade

Yields 1 cup/250 mL

1 cup	black olives, pitted	240 mL
1 clove	garlic, minced	1 clove
1 Tbsp	capers, rinsed	15 mL
2	anchovy fillets, chopped	2
3 Tbsp	olive oil	45 mL
1 Tbsp	lemon juice	15 mL
1 Tbsp	chopped fresh parsley	15 mL

We use this condiment with grilled lamb and crisp eggplant; it also works well with tuna in a niçoise salad.

PLACE THE OLIVES, garlic, capers and anchovies in a food processor and pulse to chop them. Add the olive oil and lemon juice and pulse to blend. Transfer the tapenade to a small bowl and add the parsley. Will keep refrigerated in an airtight container for up to 4 days.

Red Wine Sauce

Yields 3 cups/750 mL

1 Tbsp	grapeseed oil	15 mL
3	shallots, sliced	3
1 clove	garlic, sliced	1 clove
⅔ cup	Marsala wine	150 mL
1 cup	red wine	250 mL
1 sprig	fresh thyme	1 sprig
4 cups	veal demi-glace (page 234)	1 L

This sauce is perfect with red meats or any pan-fried peppered steaks.

HEAT THE GRAPESEED oil in a medium saucepan on medium heat. Add the shallots and garlic and sauté until soft and slightly caramelized, about 4 minutes. Add the Marsala and red wines and the thyme, then reduce the sauce to almost a thin syrup, about 10 minutes. Stir in the veal demi-glace and continue cooking until the sauce coats the back of a spoon, about 8 minutes. Season with salt and pepper. Strain the sauce through a fine-mesh sieve or a cheesecloth into a clean bowl, discarding any solids. Will keep refrigerated in an airtight container for up to 1 week.

Simple Syrup

Yields 3 cups/750 mL

2 cups	water	500 mL
2 cups	granulated sugar	480 mL

PLACE THE WATER and sugar in a small saucepan and whisk to combine. Cook on medium heat until the mixture comes to a boil and the sugar is dissolved. Remove from the heat and refrigerate for 45 minutes, until chilled. Will keep refrigerated in an airtight container for up to 2 weeks.

Brandied Cherries

Yields 3 cups/700 mL

4 ½ cups	pitted cherries (such as lapin or Bing)	1 L
2 cups	simple syrup (page 239)	500 mL
½ cup	brandy	125 mL
1	vanilla bean, pod split and seeds scraped	1

This a great way to preserve cherries and they go especially well with Black Forest cake.

PLACE ALL OF the ingredients in a medium saucepan on medium-low heat and cook until the cherries soften and the liquid is slightly thickened, about 10 minutes. Remove the brandied cherries from the heat, transfer them to a bowl and refrigerate until chilled, about 45 minutes. Will keep refrigerated in an airtight container for up to 2 weeks.

Dried Fruit Chips

Yields 15 to 20 chips

½ recipe	simple syrup (page 239)	½ recipe
	Juice of 1 lemon	
1	apple, such as Pink Lady or Granny Smith, skin on	1
	OR	
1	pear, such as Anjou, skin on	1

At the restaurant, we prepare a variety of dried fruit chips to use as garnishes for both sweet and savoury dishes. The method described below works well with apples and pears. To make pineapple chips, which don't require any additional sugar or the lemon juice, just peel the fruit then slice the flesh horizontally and bake it as for the apples and pears. Using silicone mats will result in flatter and more attractive chips, but parchment paper will work just as well.

PREHEAT THE OVEN to 185°F/85°C. Line two baking sheets with silicone baking mats or parchment paper.

Place the simple syrup in a small saucepan and bring it to a boil on high heat. Remove from the heat and add the lemon juice. Set the syrup aside in a warm place.

To make apple chips, cut the apple in half horizontally. To make pear chips, cut the pear in half vertically. Using a mandoline or a tough, very sharp knife, begin on the cut side and slice the fruit as thinly as possible. (Don't worry about the core or the seeds, as a sharp blade will slice right through them. The seed pattern gives the chips a nice design.) Cut 5 to 6 pieces, then submerge them in the warm lemon syrup, swirling them gently with a fork or spoon. Continue slicing and submerging the fruit, in batches if necessary to prevent overcrowding the saucepan.

When the fruit is well saturated and slightly translucent, 5 to 10 minutes, remove one slice at a time. Wipe any excess syrup on the edge of the saucepan, then lay each slice on the baking tray. Be sure not to overlap the fruit. Using your fingertips, gently smooth the slices so they adhere firmly to the baking mat or parchment paper.

Bake the fruit for 1½ to 2 hours, or until the chips are leathery while still warm but harden quickly when gently peeled off the tray. Carefully peel all of the chips from the tray and allow them to cool.

Will keep in an airtight container at room temperature for up to 1 week.

Sushi Rice

Serves 4 (Yields about 4 rolls)

1 cup	uncooked sushi rice	240 mL
1 cup	water	250 mL
2 Tbsp	rice wine vinegar	30 mL
2 Tbsp	granulated sugar	30 mL
1 tsp	salt	5 mL

We use this recipe for all the sushi we prepare at the Raw Bar.

PLACE THE RICE and water in a large bowl. Wash the rice by swirling it in water and pressing it against the bowl in circular motions. Use a sieve to drain the rice. Repeat this rinsing and draining process until the excess starch is gone and the water runs clear. Drain the rice one last time, removing as much water as possible.

Transfer the rice to a rice cooker and add the 1 cup/250 mL of clean water. Set the machine to "cook." Once the rice is cooked, the switch will turn to "keep warm." Allow the rice to rest in this "keep warm" mode for 10 more minutes.

While the rice is resting, prepare the sushi-zu. In a small non-reactive saucepan on medium heat, combine the rice wine vinegar, sugar and salt and bring them to a boil, then remove from the heat.

Scoop the rice into a large wooden bowl. Sprinkle the sushi-zu over the rice. Using a rice paddle, fold the sushi-zu into the rice using cutting motions and being careful not to crush the rice grains. Once the sushi-zu is fully incorporated, fan the rice with a magazine or a fan to cool it off as quickly as possible.

Remember to always have your hands and surfaces slightly damp when touching sushi rice to keep it from sticking.

Fresh Pasta Dough

Yields 1 ⅛ lbs/500 g

6½ oz	eggs (about 4 large)	185 g
4 oz	egg yolks (about 5 large)	115 g
1 Tbsp	olive oil	15 mL
1⅛ lbs	Italian "oo" flour	500 g
1 tsp	salt	5 mL

The "oo" flour is durum wheat flour that works very well for pasta and gnocchi and is readily available in grocery stores. If you cannot find it, substitute all-purpose flour.

COMBINE THE EGGS, egg yolks and olive oil in a large bowl and mix gently with a fork to break the yolks.

Place the flour and salt in a food processor and blend for 10 seconds to aerate them. With the machine running, slowly pour in the egg mixture and process just until combined.

Turn the dough out onto a clean work surface. Bring the dough together with your hands and knead it for 5 to 7 minutes until it is smooth. Wrap the dough in plastic wrap and allow it to rest for 30 minutes before using. Will keep tightly wrapped in plastic wrap and refrigerated for up to 2 days.

Brioche

Yields 2 loaves (each 5 × 9 inches/12.5 × 22.5 cm)

⅞ oz	fresh yeast	25 g
1 Tbsp	lukewarm water	15 mL
11 oz	unsalted butter, cold (about 1⅓ cups/320 mL)	310 g
6	large eggs, cold	6
18 oz	all-purpose flour, sifted (about 2¼ cups/560 mL)	500 g
½ oz	salt (about 1 Tbsp/15 mL)	15 g
1¾ oz	granulated sugar (about ¼ cup/60 mL)	50 g

CRUMBLE THE YEAST into the bowl of an electric mixer. Add the water and mix by hand to thoroughly moisten.

Cut the butter into 1-inch/2.5-cm cubes, place them in a bowl and set the butter aside to warm slightly. You want it to be cold, but malleable.

Crack the eggs into a medium bowl and, with a fork, whisk them slightly just to break them up. Add the eggs to the yeast mixture.

In a separate bowl, combine the flour, salt and sugar and stir well. Add the dry ingredients to the yeast mixture in one addition. Fit the mixer with a paddle attachment and mix on low speed until the dough is just combined. Increase the speed to medium and add the butter cubes a few at a time. It helps to gently crush each cube with your fingers as you add it. Continue mixing the dough for 4 to 5 minutes after all of the butter has been added. The dough should be smooth, elastic and quite wet (almost unmanageable). Transfer the dough to a bowl, cover it loosely with plastic wrap and refrigerate for at least 12 hours to allow it to proof.

Preheat the oven to 360°F/180°C. Butter and flour two 5 × 9-inch/12.5 × 22.5-cm loaf pans. Lightly flour a clean work surface.

Divide the chilled dough into two equal pieces. On the floured work surface, flatten one piece of dough into a rough rectangle about 4 inches/10 cm across, 8 inches/20 cm long and about 1 inch/2.5 cm thick. Arrange the rectangle with the short edge toward you, then start at the bottom and roll the dough into a tight cylinder. Use the palm of your hand to seal the dough into itself as you roll it. Transfer the cylinder, seam side down, into one of the prepared pans. Using your knuckles, flatten the cylinder so the dough fills the bottom of the pan. Repeat with the second piece of the dough. Cover the tops of the pans with plastic wrap, then allow the dough to proof in a warm place until it almost reaches the top of the pans (it will grow 2½ to 3 times in volume), 45 minutes to 1 hour.

Bake the brioches for 30 minutes, rotating the pans after about 15 minutes. Unmould the loaves, transfer them to a wire rack and allow to cool. The loaves should be a dark golden-brown and slightly hollow-sounding when tapped on the bottom. The brioches are best used the same day but will keep, wrapped in plastic wrap, for up to 2 days or frozen for up to 10 days.

A Note about Measurements

ETRIC MEASUREMENTS for volumes vary between dry and wet ingredients, as dry ingredients settle more than wet ones do. For this reason, 1 cup in this book is sometimes 240 mL, other times 250 mL, depending on the ingredient. The conversion charts below clarify these apparent discrepancies.

DRY INGREDIENTS	
⅓ cup	80 mL
½ cup	120 mL
⅔ cup	160 mL
¾ cup	180 mL
⅞ cup	210 mL
1 cup	240 mL
1 ¼ cups	300 mL
1 ⅓ cups	320 mL
1 ½ cups	355 mL
1 ⅔ cups	400 mL
1 ¾ cups	420 mL
2 cups	480 mL
2 ¼ cups	535 mL
2 ½ cups	600 mL
2 ¾ cups	660 mL
3 cups	720 mL

WET INGREDIENTS	
⅓ cup	80 mL
½ cup	125 mL
⅔ cup	165 mL
¾ cup	185 mL
⅞ cup	220 mL
1 cup	250 mL
1 ¼ cups	315 mL
1 ⅓ cups	330 mL
1 ½ cups	375 mL
1 ⅔ cups	415 mL
1 ¾ cups	435 mL
2 cups	500 mL
2 ¼ cups	560 mL
2 ½ cups	625 mL
2 ¾ cups	690 mL
3 cups	750 mL

ARAXI 243

Acknowledgements

VERY MUCH LIKE operating our restaurants, cookbook projects are also born of strong collaborations. Following our successes with *West: The Cookbook* and *Blue Water Cafe Seafood Cookbook*, the collaboration that defines Araxi in Whistler is now chronicled in these pages.

My thanks must start with our loyal patrons, whether they be the pioneering residents of Whistler, whose zest for life is unrivalled, or our Canadian, American and overseas friends who visit us throughout the year. Because this is both a cookbook and a testament to conscientious choices in dining, we thank every individual who has, by sharing the experience at Araxi, supported the decisions made by chef James Walt, and, by extension, supported the day-by-day effort to sustain responsible growing, ranching and fishery practices.

Led by James, our talented kitchen brigade continues to explore the exceptional ingredients of Pemberton Valley farms and ranches, and our coastal fishery. My sincere thanks to James, Aaron Heath, Tim Pickwell (who has been with us for the 28-year lifetime of the restaurant), John Ferris, Victor Pulleyblank, Mike Guy, Steve Edwards, Rene Wuethrich, Alia Daut-Labesse, Samantha Rahn, Pat Allan, Megan Cochrane and Scot Curry.

Of the many alumni of Araxi, I would like to signal the efforts of Neil Henderson, Brian Hopkins, Chris Van Nus, Bradley Fraser and Andrew Richardson. I would also like to thank Shelley McArthur and Lawrence Fung from Top Table, and the late Werner Forster, whose legacy lies in the design of Araxi.

Many thanks go to the talented, first-rate team at Douglas & McIntyre, notably Chris Labonté, Peter Cocking, Naomi MacDougall and Lucy Kenward. As in our first two books, the restaurant has been brought to life with John Sherlock's brilliant photography and Jim Tobler's eloquent writing.

A friend once said that we were put on this earth to bring out the best in other people, so that they may bring out the best in us. So now I thank my most important collaborator: my first love, Araxi, my wife who so graciously worked with me to establish this restaurant.

Jack Evrensel

Index